Merry Christmas
to the Kinnells.
Love,
Genieva 2004

Woodland Bible Stories

Alan & Linda Parry

Abingdon Press

Published in the United States of America by Abingdon Press
201 Eighth Avenue South
Nashville, TN 37203

Printed in Singapore

Contents

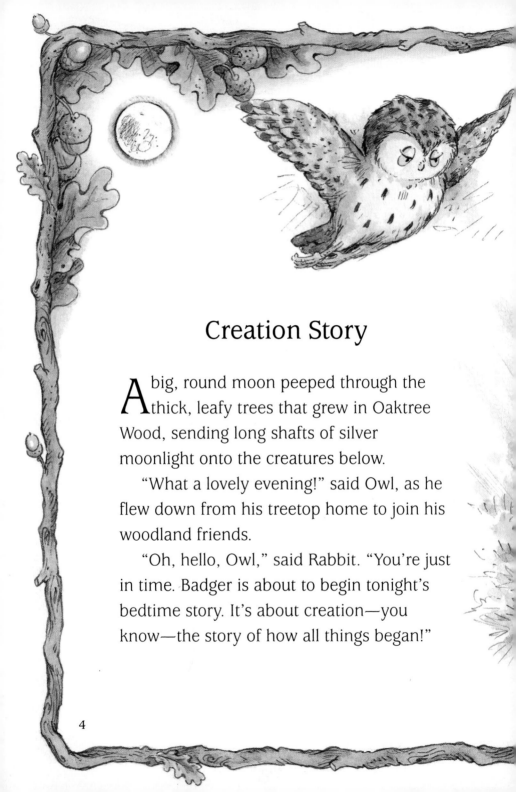

Creation Story

A big, round moon peeped through the
thick, leafy trees that grew in Oaktree
Wood, sending long shafts of silver
moonlight onto the creatures below.

"What a lovely evening!" said Owl, as he
flew down from his treetop home to join his
woodland friends.

"Oh, hello, Owl," said Rabbit. "You're just
in time. Badger is about to begin tonight's
bedtime story. It's about creation—you
know—the story of how all things began!"

"In the beginning God made the stars and the planets," said Badger. "Then He looked down upon the earth and said,

'Let there be light!' And the sun shone down and warmed the earth. When the earth felt the warm, gentle heat from the sun, flowers and trees began to grow.

Genesis 1:1-13.

Say a prayer with Owl:
Lord, thank you for the millions and millions of twinkling stars.

Let's think…
Look—look up into the sky,
And see the stars above,
Do you know the one who made them?
Do you know about His love?

Next, God made seas and rivers and filled them with fish and all sorts of creatures that like to live in the water. Then He made the birds and animals.

Last of all, God took some clay and made it into the shape of a man. Then He breathed into the man and he became alive. God called the man, Adam.

Genesis 1:20-25. 2:7.

Sing with all the woodland animals:

All things bright and beautiful,
All creatures great and small,
All things wise and wonderful,
The Lord God made them all.

(C. F. Alexander 1823-95)

Say a prayer with Mole:

Thank you, Lord, for everything you have made.

7

God made a garden for Adam to live in. It was called, 'The Garden of Eden.' Two special trees, 'The Tree that gives Life' and 'The Tree of Good and Bad' grew in the garden.

'Do not eat the fruit from the Tree of Good and Bad,' said God. 'Or you will die!'

Genesis 2:8-9,15-17.

Say a prayer with Deer:
*Lord, let your words
be important to me
so that I won't forget them.*

Let's think…
How many types of fruit can you think of that grow on trees?

'It is not good for Adam to be alone,' said God. So the Lord brought to Adam all the creatures that He had made, and Adam gave each of them a name.

But nowhere could Adam find anyone who was just like himself, and before long he began to feel very lonely.

Genesis 2:18-20.

Mouse says:
Whenever I get lonely,
Upset, or just real sad,
I ask the one who loves me,
To help me to be glad.

Let's think…
Do you sometimes feel lonely?

9

Suddenly, Adam felt very tired and he fell into a deep sleep. While he slept, God took out one of his ribs and closed up the flesh. Then, out of the rib, God made a woman and brought her to Adam.

'At last, here is one of my own kind,' said Adam. 'Her bones come from my bones, her body comes from my body. I will call her 'woman' because she was taken out of man.'

Genesis 2:21-23.

Rabbit says:
Thank you for giving Adam a friend, Lord.

Let's think…
Have you got a friend? Do you think it's good to have friends?

The man and woman did not wear
any clothes, for they did not think it
was wrong.

Every day they worked in the garden that
they loved, making it even prettier. And every
day they gathered the berries and fruit from the
trees and ate them together by the riverside.

Genesis 2:25,15-16.

Badger says:

Lord, you are the reason
The flowers smell sweet,
Why the brown leaves rustle
Beneath my feet.

Let's think…Have you ever trod on dry, brown leaves, making
that lovely crunchy sound?

11

Then one day, a strange creature, called a serpent, came into the garden.

'Has God said that you can't eat from every tree in the garden?' it asked Eve.

'That's right,' said Eve. 'We can eat from all of the trees in the garden, except from the Tree of Good and Bad. God said we must not eat that fruit, or we'll die!'

Genesis 3:1-3.

Say a prayer with Squirrel:
Lord, give me strength to choose what is right.

Let's think…
Sometimes we want to do wrong things—why do you think that is?

'You won't die!' cried the serpent. 'God only said that because He knows that when you eat it, you will be wise like gods, knowing good and bad.'

So Eve, who had always wanted to be wise and clever, took some of the fruit and ate it. Then she gave some to Adam, and he ate it.

Genesis 3:4-6.

Say a prayer with Fox:
Help me Lord, to say no to bad things.

Let's think…
The snake tricked Eve. Do you think that was kind?

Suddenly, Adam and Eve knew that they were naked. Quickly, they sewed some fig leaves together to make aprons.

That evening, when they heard God walking in the garden, they ran and hid from Him among the trees.

'Where are you?' called God. 'Why are you hiding?'

'We are afraid,' Adam called, 'because we are naked!'

Genesis 3:7-10.

Say a prayer with Mouse:
Let me never want to hide from you, Lord.

Let's think…
If God walked in your garden would you hide from Him?

'Who told you that you are naked?'
asked God. 'Have you eaten the fruit I told
you not to eat?'

'Eve gave it to me!' cried Adam.

'It was the serpent,' cried Eve. 'It tricked me!'
Then God punished the serpent.

'You will crawl on your belly and eat dust, for
as long as you live!' He said.

Genesis 3:11-14.

Mole says:

*Lord, help me to own up if
I do something wrong.*

Do you know?
It is thought that long ago,
snakes had legs! And pythons
and boa constrictors still have
hip bones!

After that, God made some clothes from animal skins for Adam and Eve. Then He sent them out of the garden in case they should eat the fruit from The Tree that gives Life, and live for ever. God put angels and a flaming sword in the garden to guard it.

Genesis 3:21-24.

Say a prayer with Badger:
Help me to remember that everything you do, Lord, is for our own good. Amen.

Let's think…
Has anyone ever said to you, "It's for your own good"?

Now life was difficult for Adam and Eve. They had to work hard to grow their food and to make their clothes. But before long, their first two sons were born. They were called Cain and Abel.

When they grew up, Cain became a farmer and Abel became a shepherd.

Genesis 3:17-19. 4:1-2.

Say a prayer with all the little mice children:

When we grow up, Lord, help us to choose the jobs that you want us to do.

Let's think…

How many jobs can you think of that grown up people do?

17

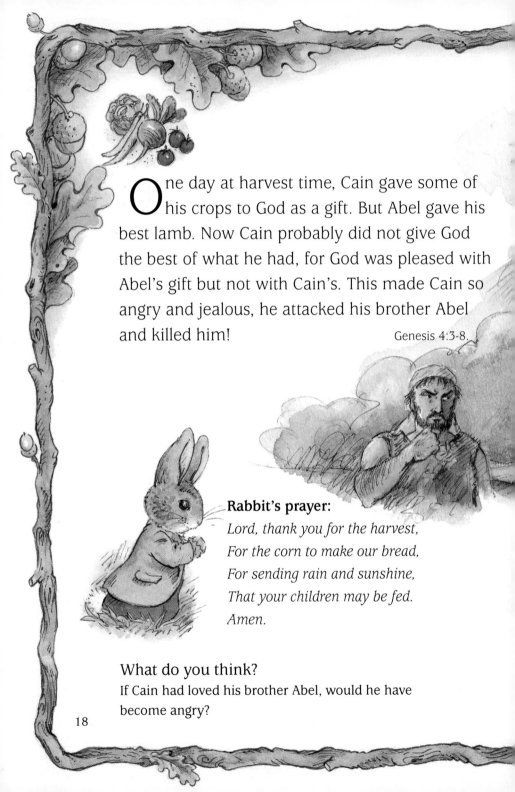

One day at harvest time, Cain gave some of his crops to God as a gift. But Abel gave his best lamb. Now Cain probably did not give God the best of what he had, for God was pleased with Abel's gift but not with Cain's. This made Cain so angry and jealous, he attacked his brother Abel and killed him!

Genesis 4:3-8.

Rabbit's prayer:

Lord, thank you for the harvest,
For the corn to make our bread,
For sending rain and sunshine,
That your children may be fed.
Amen.

What do you think?

If Cain had loved his brother Abel, would he have become angry?

'Where is your brother, Abel?
God asked Cain.

'I don't know,' said Cain. 'Am I my
brother's keeper?'

But the Lord knew what Cain had done.
'Because you have killed your brother, you
must leave your home and your family,' He
said. 'From now on, you will be a homeless
wanderer on the earth.'

Genesis 4:9-12.

Say a prayer with Owl:
Lord, take away my anger,
Let me not get mad,
For those who dislike others
Make you very sad.

Let's think…
We can't 'pretend' to God.

In time, Adam and Eve had more children, and their children grew up and had families of their own. And so, the number of people on earth grew and grew.

But when God looked down upon them, he was not pleased, because the people were bad. But there was one man who loved God and did what was right. His name was Noah."

Genesis 5:3-32. 6:1-8.

Lord, keep us safe this night
And take away our fears,
May angels guard us while we sleep,
Till morning light appears.

(Traditional)

When Badger had at last finished
reading the creation story, it was time for
all the mummies and daddies to put their
children to bed.

The bright, silver moon smiled down on them
and seemed to say,

"Goodnight, everyone! Sleep tight!"

Noah

The insects buzzed lazily as the hot midsummer sun shone brightly down through the leaves in Oaktree Wood.

All the woodland creatures who lived in the wood had decided to take a picnic down to the riverside where it was cool.

Mouse and Mole pulled off their shoes and socks and dangled their feet in the water.

After they had eaten, Water Vole took some of them for a ride in her boat. There were so many animals on board, Mouse quite thought they were going to sink!

"Ho! Ho!" laughed Badger. "This reminds me of a story I know. It is about a lot of animals and a boat and a man named Noah…"

"Noah was the great, great, great, great, great, great, great, grandson of Adam," began Badger. "He was a good man who loved God, but all the other people around him were bad. They lived wicked lives and thought about evil things all the time.

Luke 4:36-38.

Badger says:
Whatever is lovely,
Whatever is true,
Let's think about these things
All our life through.

Let's think...
If you are filled up with good things, there won't be any space left for bad things!

When God looked down upon the
world and saw how bad the people were,
He said,
   'I will wipe out these people that I have
       created, because I am sorry that I ever
          made them!'

Genesis 6:5-9.

Say a prayer with Mole:
Lord, let me never make you sorry,
but if I do, help me to be sorry, too.

Let's remember…
God is the Great One—the Great Creator. He always knows best.

25

B ut God was pleased with Noah, and He said, 'Noah, I am going to wash away all the bad things on the earth with a great flood. Everything that is evil will be destroyed! But I will save you and your wife and your three sons and their wives.

Genesis 6:13,17-18.

Rabbit says:

Whenever I feel naughty,
And want to do what's wrong,
I quickly ask the Great One,
To make me good and strong.

Owl's prayer:

Help me to remember, Lord, that if ever I do anything
wrong, I only have to say sorry and you will forgive me.

I want you to build an Ark, which
will be like a very big boat,' God told Noah.

'Make it 140 metres long, 23 metres wide
and 13.5 metres high. Make a window all the
way around the Ark 0.5 metres below the roof.

'Build three decks inside the Ark, a bottom,
middle and upper deck, and put a door in the side.'

Genesis 6:14-16.

Squirrel says:
Lord, thank you that Noah obeyed you.

Just imagine…
What a huge project building the Ark must have been. It was longer
than a football field and bigger, even, than a navy destroyer!

Noah and his sons began to build the Ark. Their friends and neighbors laughed.

'We're miles from the sea,' they cried. 'What's the use of having a boat on dry land?'

'God is going to send a great flood on the earth,' Noah explained. 'Everyone who is bad will be washed away! But if you turn to God and do what is right, then you will be saved!'

Genesis 6:22.

Say a prayer with Mole:

Lord, sometimes others laugh at me
For following your way,
Let them not upset me
No matter what they say.

Let's think…

Do we ever laugh at others for doing what is right?

'What—a great flood here! This land has never flooded!' cried the people. 'You're balmy!'

But Noah and his sons kept on building the Ark. It took them many, many years and all that time Noah taught the people, hoping that they would turn from their bad ways and ask God to forgive them, and so save them from the flood.

2 Peter 2:5.

Can you sing this action rhyme with Rabbit?:
Build, build, build the Ark, up, up high,
Build, build, build the Ark up to the sky.
Hammer, hammer, hammer the nails, one,
*   two, three,*
Noah built the Ark, for all to see.

Let's think…Some jobs take a very long time, but if we stick to them, they will get finished.

29

When the Ark was finished, Noah painted it with tar to make it watertight.

Then God said, 'Bring a pair of every animal into the Ark to keep them safe from the flood. But bring seven pairs of every type of animal that is good to eat for food.

Take your whole family with you,' said God.

Genesis 6:14,19-20.

Owl's prayer:

Lord, thank you for the Ark,
A great big floating house,
With space for woodland creatures
Like Badger, Mole and Mouse.

Let's think...

Do you know what else God told Noah to store in the Ark?

'For I can see that you are the only one in all the world who does what is right!'

So Noah, his wife and their three sons, Shem, Ham and Japheth and their wives went into the Ark. Then all of the animals came, two by two. They all went into the Ark with Noah.

Then the Lord God shut the door behind them.

Genesis 7:1-3,13-16.

Say a rhyme with Mouse:

Come lions and tigers,
Giraffes and bears,
Come monkeys and cats and aardvark,
Come hippos and warthogs,
Donkeys and pigs,
There is room for you all in the Ark!

Let's think…
How many pairs of chickens went into the Ark?

31

As soon as everyone was safe inside the Ark,
big, black clouds began to darken the sky.
Water gushed up from underground wells beneath
the earth and the rain fell down in torrents for forty
days and nights.

Genesis 7:11-12.

Say a rhyme with Squirrel:

*Higher and higher
The waters rose,
Even higher than the trees.
The rain fell down
And the floods went up,
And the Ark rose up with ease.*

What do you think was happening inside the Ark?

Water lapped against the sides of the Ark. Then suddenly, the great boat began to float! It went up and up as the waters rose higher and higher.

It went up so high, it rose even higher than the tallest mountain!

Higher and higher
The water rose,
Even higher than each hill.
The rain fell down,
And the floods went up,
But the Ark is floating still!

Genesis 7:17-20.

Let's think…
Have you ever been for a ride in a boat?

33

But God did not forget Noah and his family and all the animals in the Ark, and after 150 days He made a strong wind blow on the waters and the flood began to go down. The underground wells closed up and the rain stopped. Then, seven months after the rain began, the Ark came to rest on the mountains of Ararat.

Genesis 8:1-4.

Say a prayer with Water Vole:
Lord, you don't forget,
Those who trust in you,
Your love shines down upon them,
Faithful, kind and true.

Let's think…
Do you think Noah and his family were busy in the Ark? What do you think they had to do for the animals?

'Look!' said Noah. 'Now we can see the tops of the mountains! The flood must be going down!'

Forty days later, Noah wanted to find out if the water had gone right down (he couldn't see the ground from the top of Mount Ararat). So he opened a window and let out a dove, but the dove could not find a place to land, so it flew back to the Ark. Noah reached out his arm and took it in. The earth was still not dry.

Genesis 8:5-9.

Mouse prays:

Lord, teach me to trust
In your loving care,
For though I can't see you,
I know you are there.

Let's think…

What would have happened if Noah had been impatient and let the animals out too soon?

Seven days later, Noah sent out the dove again. This time it came back with a fresh olive leaf in its beak. The water had almost gone from the earth! Seven days after that, Noah sent out the dove again and this time it did not return. The earth was dry!

Genesis 8:10-12

Say a prayer with Owl:
All things are possible with you, Lord.
And without you we can do nothing.

Let's think…
What do you think happened to the dove?

Then God said to Noah,

'It is time for you and your family to leave the Ark. Let the birds and animals go free so that they can have babies and fill the earth.'

And so, eleven months after they had gone into the Ark, Noah threw off the covering and opened the door. Then everyone ran out into God's new world.

Genesis 8:13-19.

Say a rhyme with all the woodland friends:

The earth is good,
It's made anew,
Ready, waiting
For me and you!

Vole's prayer:

Thank you, Lord, that the earth is filled with life.

37

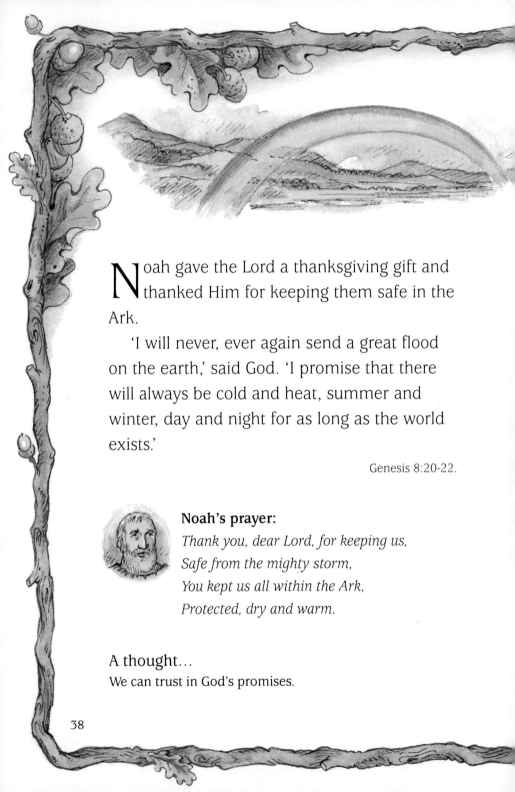

N oah gave the Lord a thanksgiving gift and thanked Him for keeping them safe in the Ark.

'I will never, ever again send a great flood on the earth,' said God. 'I promise that there will always be cold and heat, summer and winter, day and night for as long as the world exists.'

Genesis 8:20-22.

Noah's prayer:
Thank you, dear Lord, for keeping us,
Safe from the mighty storm,
You kept us all within the Ark,
Protected, dry and warm.

A thought…
We can trust in God's promises.

Then God put a beautiful
rainbow in the sky.

'Whenever I see the rainbow
appear in the sky,' said God, 'I will
remember my promise to you and all the
animals!'

And that is the end of the story," said Badger.

"Oh, help!" cried Mouse. "We're sinking!"

Water Vole rowed the animals back to
shore.

"Ho, ho!" laughed Badger, as he helped
Vole bale out. "I think we had too many on
board!"

"Yes, I'm afraid my boat is not quite as
big as the Ark!" chuckled Vole.

Genesis 9:8-17.

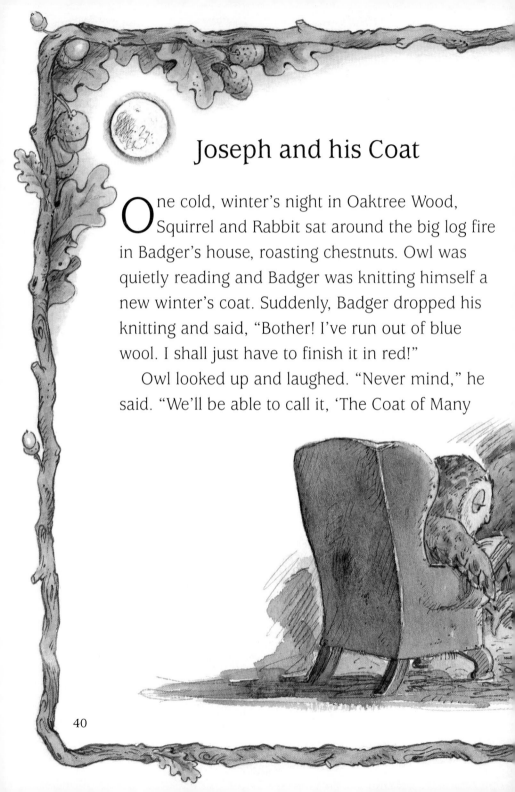

Joseph and his Coat

One cold, winter's night in Oaktree Wood, Squirrel and Rabbit sat around the big log fire in Badger's house, roasting chestnuts. Owl was quietly reading and Badger was knitting himself a new winter's coat. Suddenly, Badger dropped his knitting and said, "Bother! I've run out of blue wool. I shall just have to finish it in red!"

Owl looked up and laughed. "Never mind," he said. "We'll be able to call it, 'The Coat of Many

Colors,' like Joseph's in the Bible!"

"What was that?" asked Rabbit, as he tried to peel a hot chestnut. "What was that you said about Joseph?"

"You know, the story about Joseph's coat in the Bible!" said Owl.

"No, I don't know that one!" said Rabbit. "Will you tell it to us, Owl? Please!"

"Oh, very well," said Owl…

"Jacob had twelve sons. He loved them all, of course," began Owl, "but Joseph, who was number eleven, was his favorite.

When he was seventeen years old, Jacob made Joseph a special robe—a coat of many colors. Joseph wore it all the time. It made him feel really important.

His brothers were furious.

Genesis 35:22-26. 37:1-4.

Badger says:
The Lord has no favorites,
So we can all share,
His love and his kindness,
His warm, Father care.

Did you know?
Joseph was a descendant of Shem—one of the sons of Noah who went into the Ark!

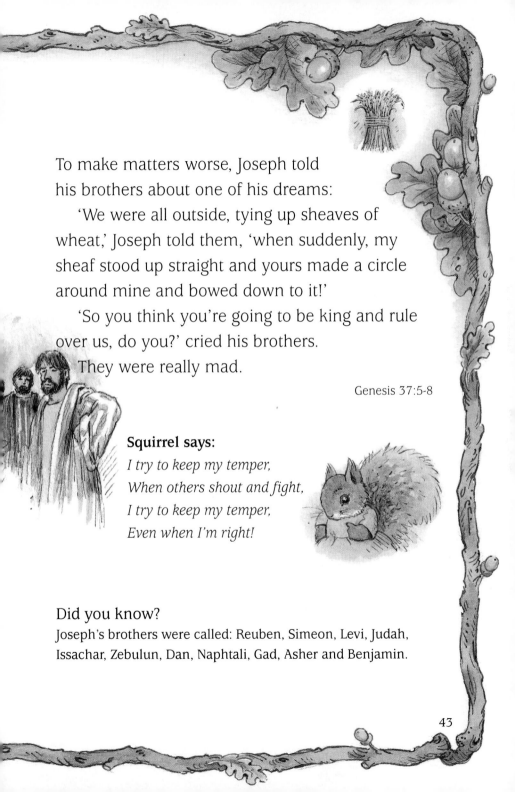

To make matters worse, Joseph told
his brothers about one of his dreams:

'We were all outside, tying up sheaves of
wheat,' Joseph told them, 'when suddenly, my
sheaf stood up straight and yours made a circle
around mine and bowed down to it!'

'So you think you're going to be king and rule
over us, do you?' cried his brothers.

They were really mad.

Genesis 37:5-8

Squirrel says:

I try to keep my temper,
When others shout and fight,
I try to keep my temper,
Even when I'm right!

Did you know?
Joseph's brothers were called: Reuben, Simeon, Levi, Judah,
Issachar, Zebulun, Dan, Naphtali, Gad, Asher and Benjamin.

Soon, Joseph had another dream. He just couldn't keep quiet about it.

'I saw the sun and moon and eleven stars bowing down to me!' he boasted.

Even Jacob got mad when he heard about it.

'What—do you think that even your mother and father as well as your brothers are going to bow down to you?' he said.

Genesis 37:9-11.

Rabbit says:

Help me not to brag, dear Lord,
In big or little ways,
For you teach your little ones
That boasting never pays.

Let's think…
Do you know anyone who boasts?

Then one day, Jacob sent Joseph out into the countryside to check up on his brothers who were looking after the sheep and goats.

'Here comes that dreamer,' they said, when they saw Joseph coming. 'Let's kill him and throw his body in a pit—no one will ever find out!'

'Let's not kill him,' said Reuben. 'Just throw him into the pit—but don't harm him!' Then he went off to tend the sheep, but on his return he planned to rescue Joseph and send him back to his father.

When Joseph showed up, the brothers ripped off his coat and threw him into the pit.

Genesis 37:12-24.

Let's think…

Being jealous and angry can lead us to do awful things. Can you remember what Jesus said about being angry?

(Matthew 5:21-24)

45

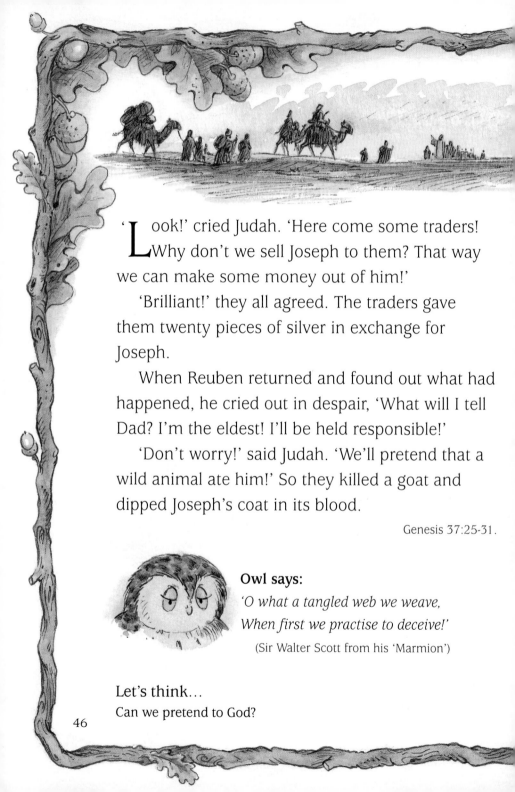

'Look!' cried Judah. 'Here come some traders! Why don't we sell Joseph to them? That way we can make some money out of him!'

'Brilliant!' they all agreed. The traders gave them twenty pieces of silver in exchange for Joseph.

When Reuben returned and found out what had happened, he cried out in despair, 'What will I tell Dad? I'm the eldest! I'll be held responsible!'

'Don't worry!' said Judah. 'We'll pretend that a wild animal ate him!' So they killed a goat and dipped Joseph's coat in its blood.

Genesis 37:25-31.

Owl says:
*'O what a tangled web we weave,
When first we practise to deceive!'*
(Sir Walter Scott from his 'Marmion')

Let's think…
Can we pretend to God?

They showed the blood-stained garment to their father.

'Do you recognize this coat?' they asked.

'Oh, yes!' cried Jacob. 'It's Joseph's! Some wild animal has attacked him and torn him to pieces!'

Jacob wept and wept. He was full of sadness and nobody could comfort him.

Genesis 37:32-35.

When Squirrel is sad, she says:
Lord, look down from heaven,
Comfort me, I pray,
Wrap your arms around me,
Wipe my tears away.

Let's think…

Have you ever lost somebody that you loved?

Meanwhile, in Egypt, the traders had sold Joseph to Potiphar, captain of the palace guard. But God was watching over Joseph, so that everything he did turned out well. Potiphar saw this, and soon put Joseph in charge of his entire household and everything he owned.

Genesis 39:1-5.

Badger says:
If ever trouble comes to me,
In daytime or at night,
I know my heavenly Father
Can make everything all right.

Let's think…
All things work together for good to those who love God…

(Romans 8:28)

Potiphar's wife thought Joseph was a handsome young fellow, and one day she caught him by his coat and tried to kiss him. But Joseph knew that it was wrong to kiss another man's wife, so he ran off, leaving his coat behind.

This made Potiphar's wife really mad.

'Joseph tried to kiss me!' she lied to her husband.

Potiphar was furious and had Joseph thrown into jail.

Genesis 39:6-20.

Rabbit says:
Lord, let me be quick
To do what you say,
To run from badness
When it comes my way.

Let's think…
Do you always do what you know to be right?

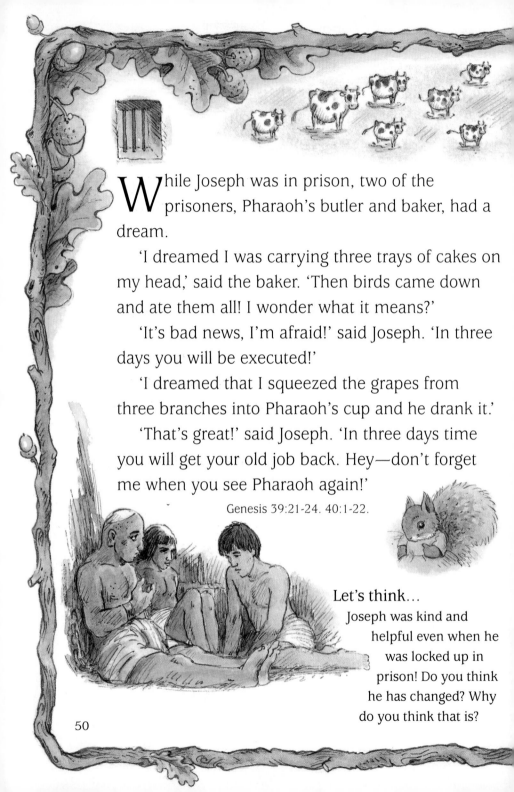

While Joseph was in prison, two of the prisoners, Pharaoh's butler and baker, had a dream.

'I dreamed I was carrying three trays of cakes on my head,' said the baker. 'Then birds came down and ate them all! I wonder what it means?'

'It's bad news, I'm afraid!' said Joseph. 'In three days you will be executed!'

'I dreamed that I squeezed the grapes from three branches into Pharaoh's cup and he drank it.'

'That's great!' said Joseph. 'In three days time you will get your old job back. Hey—don't forget me when you see Pharaoh again!'

Genesis 39:21-24. 40:1-22.

Let's think…
Joseph was kind and helpful even when he was locked up in prison! Do you think he has changed? Why do you think that is?

But the butler did forget Joseph—for two whole years—until Pharaoh had a strange dream.

'I dreamed I saw seven fat cows followed by seven thin ones,' said Pharaoh. 'They were coming up out of the river. Then the thin cows ate up the fat cows! What can it mean?'

But nobody knew. No one could work it out.

Then suddenly, the butler remembered. 'I know someone who would know the answer!' he told Pharaoh.

Genesis 40:23. 41:1-13

Let's think…
Broken promises make people sad.

51

Quickly, Joseph was brought out of prison and sent to the palace. When he heard Pharaoh's dream, he knew the meaning right away.

'The seven fat cows mean that Egypt is going to have seven years of good harvests when there will be plenty of food,' said Joseph. 'But after that no food will grow in Egypt or the surrounding countries for seven years! That's what the seven thin cows mean!'

'Dear me!' said Pharaoh. 'What shall I do?'

'You must choose a man to organize the storage of food through the seven good years, so that there will be enough to eat in the bad years,' Joseph told him.

Genesis 41:14-36.

Let's think...
How does someone become wise? The first step is to trust and respect the Lord! (Proverbs 1:7)

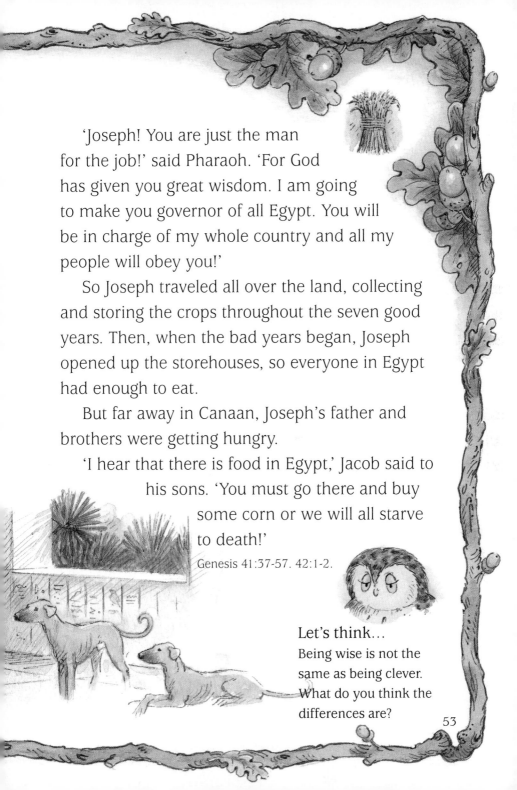

'Joseph! You are just the man
for the job!' said Pharaoh. 'For God
has given you great wisdom. I am going
to make you governor of all Egypt. You will
be in charge of my whole country and all my
people will obey you!'

So Joseph traveled all over the land, collecting
and storing the crops throughout the seven good
years. Then, when the bad years began, Joseph
opened up the storehouses, so everyone in Egypt
had enough to eat.

But far away in Canaan, Joseph's father and
brothers were getting hungry.

'I hear that there is food in Egypt,' Jacob said to
his sons. 'You must go there and buy
some corn or we will all starve
to death!'

Genesis 41:37-57. 42:1-2.

Let's think...
Being wise is not the
same as being clever.
What do you think the
differences are?

53

So Jacob's sons traveled to Egypt to buy corn. They came to Joseph, the governor of the land, and bowed low before him. They did not recognize their brother, the boy they had sold into slavery twenty-two years earlier.

Joseph decided to test them, to see if they had changed.

'What are you foreigners doing here?' he said sternly. 'You could be spies for all I know!'

'We're not spies!' they said. 'We come from one family back in Canaan, where our father lives and our youngest brother, Benjamin.'

Genesis 42:3-13

Let's think…Do you remember Joseph's dream? Have you ever heard the saying, "We reap what we sow?"

54

'Then you must prove your story,' said Joseph. 'Or I will lock you all up in prison! You must bring me your youngest brother, Benjamin!'

A few months later, the brothers needed to go to Egypt again for food.

'We must take Benjamin,' they told their father.

'Keep him safe,' said Jacob. 'I couldn't bear it if I lost another son!'

But after Joseph had given them more corn, he hid his own silver cup in Benjamin's sack.

Genesis 42:14-38. 43. 44:1-2.

Say a prayer with Owl:
Sometimes, dear Lord, you test us,
To see what we will do,
Help us not to let you down,
But prove, that we love you.

'Someone has stolen my master's cup!' said Joseph's servant.

'What?' cried the brothers.

'Benjamin must become our slave!' said the servant, when he found the cup in Benjamin's sack.

The brothers tore their clothes in sorrow, and went back to see Joseph.

'Please, don't take away Benjamin. It will break our father's heart,' said Judah. 'Let me be your slave instead!'

Then Joseph knew that his brothers had changed and were sorry for what they had done to him.

Genesis 44:3-34.

Owl says:

Remember, everything will turn out right in the end!

56

At last, Joseph told his brothers
who he really was.

'Don't you recognize me?' he cried.
'I'm Joseph!'

But the brothers were afraid. They could not
believe it.

'Don't be frightened!' said Joseph. 'God
planned it this way so that many people would be
saved, and that you and your families might
survive. Now all of you must come and live with
me in Egypt, where I can look after you, for there
are still five more years of famine to come.'

So the brothers went home and
brought their families, their
cattle and their father Jacob
to Egypt, where Joseph
took care of them all."

Genesis 45. 46. 47:1-12.

"Well, that was a
good story," said Badger.
"But I hope my coat won't
get me into as much trouble
as Joseph's did!"

Moses

One fine morning in Oaktree Wood, Mouse and Mole decided to visit Warren Hall, where their friend, Rabbit lived. They were chatting so much, they didn't notice they had taken the wrong path and soon they were completely lost.

"Oh, dear!" said Mouse. "We seem to be walking round and round in circles. I'm sure we've been along this part of the path before!"

"Yes, you have!" chuckled someone high above them.

It was Owl.

"Oh, hello Owl," said Mouse. "Would you show us the way to Rabbit's house? We've been wandering around in the wood for ages!"

"Yes, I've been watching you," laughed Owl. "You must feel rather like the children of Israel did—only they wandered about in the desert— shall I tell you the story on the way?"

"Oh, yes please," said Mouse and Mole together.

"It all began in Egypt," said Owl. "The children of Jacob became known as 'The children of Israel.' Their descendants lived in Egypt for 400 years, where they grew into a great nation. There were so many Israelites living Egypt that the new Pharaoh complained:

'These foreigners have grown so strong they will soon be taking over the whole country,' he said. 'So I have thought up a plan to keep their numbers down. We'll force them to work for us! They can be our slaves!'

Exodus 1.

Mole says:

When others are unkind,
In what they do and say,
I ask the Lord, the Great One,
To make everything okey.

Let's think…

What do you think it feels like to live in a strange land?

But the Israelite numbers kept growing. So Pharaoh thought up another, really wicked plan.

'Throw all the Israelite baby boys into the river!' he ordered. 'That will keep their numbers down!'

But one Israelite mother, named Jochebed, thought up a plan, too.

'I will do as Pharaoh says and put my baby in the river,' she said. 'But first I will make a little basket for him!'

Exodus 1. 2:1-3.

Say a prayer with Mouse:
Lord, I've a problem—
But I know what to do,
I'll kneel down and pray,
And give the problem to you!

Let's think...
What should we do if we are told to do something bad?

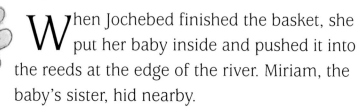

When Jochebed finished the basket, she put her baby inside and pushed it into the reeds at the edge of the river. Miriam, the baby's sister, hid nearby.

Just then, Pharaoh's daughter came down to the river to bathe. Suddenly, she saw the little basket in the reeds and sent her servant girl to fetch it.

'What a lovely baby!' cried the princess, when she peeped inside. 'I am going to keep him and bring him up as my own son!
And I shall call him, Moses!'

Exodus 2:3-6.

Owl says:
There is no need to fret,
Or to fear strife,
When you ask the Great One
To guide your life!

Let's think…
The Lord won't help us if we don't want to be helped!

Miriam came out from hiding. 'Shall I find a woman to feed the baby for you?' she asked.

'Yes, do!' said the princess.

So Miriam fetched Jochebed, the baby's own mother!

'Take care of this baby for me,' ordered the princess. 'And I will pay you well. Then, when he is old enough, bring him to me at the palace.'

Exodus 2:7-10.

Mouse says:
Trust in the Lord for a happy outcome.

Let's think…
Just how do we trust in the Lord?

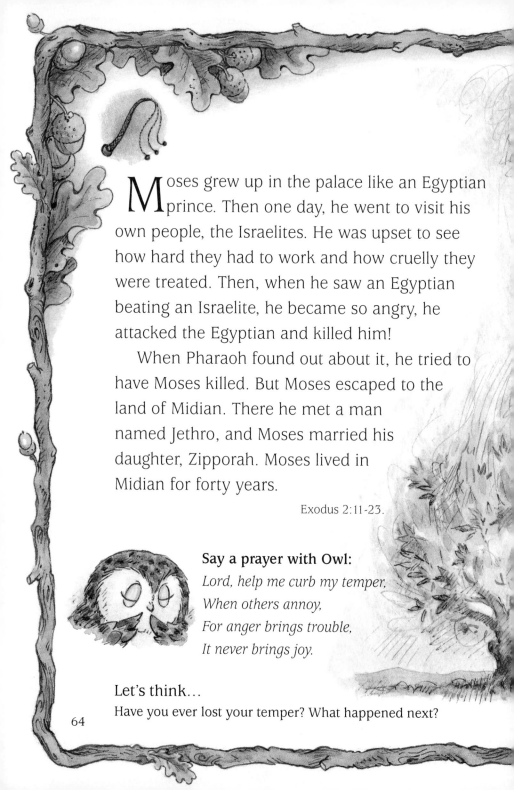

Moses grew up in the palace like an Egyptian prince. Then one day, he went to visit his own people, the Israelites. He was upset to see how hard they had to work and how cruelly they were treated. Then, when he saw an Egyptian beating an Israelite, he became so angry, he attacked the Egyptian and killed him!

When Pharaoh found out about it, he tried to have Moses killed. But Moses escaped to the land of Midian. There he met a man named Jethro, and Moses married his daughter, Zipporah. Moses lived in Midian for forty years.

Exodus 2:11-23.

Say a prayer with Owl:
Lord, help me curb my temper,
When others annoy,
For anger brings trouble,
It never brings joy.

Let's think…
Have you ever lost your temper? What happened next?

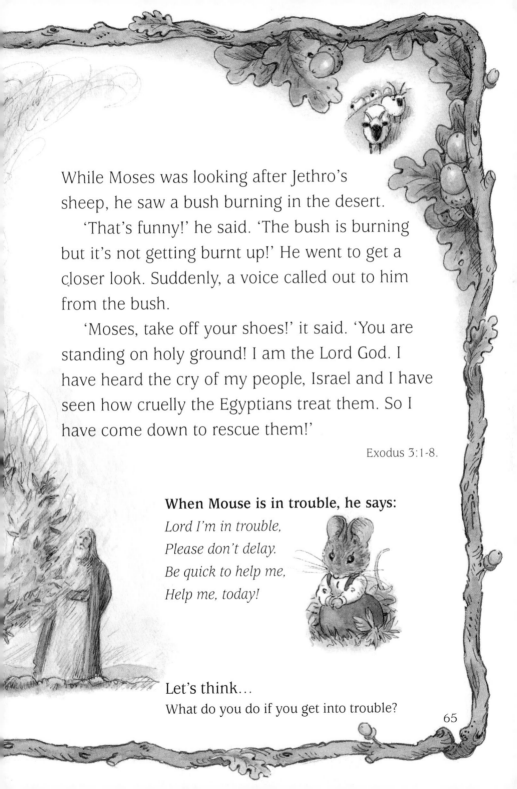

While Moses was looking after Jethro's sheep, he saw a bush burning in the desert.

'That's funny!' he said. 'The bush is burning but it's not getting burnt up!' He went to get a closer look. Suddenly, a voice called out to him from the bush.

'Moses, take off your shoes!' it said. 'You are standing on holy ground! I am the Lord God. I have heard the cry of my people, Israel and I have seen how cruelly the Egyptians treat them. So I have come down to rescue them!'

Exodus 3:1-8.

When Mouse is in trouble, he says:

Lord I'm in trouble,
Please don't delay.
Be quick to help me,
Help me, today!

Let's think...
What do you do if you get into trouble?

65

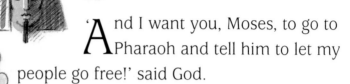

'And I want you, Moses, to go to Pharaoh and tell him to let my people go free!' said God.

'But how can I go to Pharaoh?' said Moses. 'I'm just a nobody!' 'I will be with you,' said God. ' And your brother, Aaron, will help you.'

Exodus 3:9-12. 4:14-17.

Say a prayer with Mole:
Lord, you are always with us,
No matter where we go,
You will never leave us,
Because you love us so.

Let's think…
Why do you think Moses did not want to do what God asked him?

'The Lord, the God of the
Israelites, says, "Let my people go!"'
Moses and Aaron told Pharaoh.

'No!' said Pharaoh. 'I need the Israelite
slaves to build my cities.'

Moses and Aaron kept on asking Pharaoh to let
the people go. Every time Pharaoh refused,
God punished him and all the Egyptians with
a horrible plague. It took ten plagues to make
Pharaoh give in.

Plague No. 1. The river Nile and all the
water in Egypt turned into blood.
Plague No. 2. Millions of frogs jumped
out of the rivers and hopped into the
palace and the Egyptians' homes.
They even jumped into their
beds and cooking pots!

Exodus 5:1-2. 7:14-25. 8:1-15.

Plague Nos. 3. & 4. Gnats and then flies. They flew everywhere and covered everyone and everything.

Plague No. 5. Egypt's cattle caught a terrible disease and died.

Plague No. 6. Boils and sores broke out on people and animals.

Plague No. 7. A great hailstorm flattened the crops.

Plague No. 8. A huge swarm of locusts ate up all the remaining crops.

Egypt was ruined. But still Pharaoh said, 'No!'

Exodus 8:16-10:20.

Owl says:

The Lord always gives,
A warning, I know,
Before trouble comes
On the earth below.

Let's think...

What should we do if we are warned about something?

Plague No. 9. For three days thick darkness covered the land. The Egyptians couldn't even see one another.

But through all of these plagues, God kept the children of Israel safe. Then came the last, terrible plague.

Plague No. 10. The death of the first-born. Every first-born creature, including children, died!

To escape the last plague, God told the Israelites to mark their door posts with the blood of a lamb, so that the death angel would pass over their homes, keeping their first-born safe.

Exodus 10:21-29. 11. 12:21-30.

Say a prayer with Mouse:

Lord, you protect,
Both night and day,
Those who love you
And do as you say.

Let's think...

Do we always do what our mummies and daddies say?

69

After the tenth terrible plague, Pharaoh finally gave in and let the people go.

But before they went, the Israelites collected silver and gold from their Egyptian neighbors. God gave them such favor, that whatever they asked for, the Egyptians gave them.

Exodus 12:31-36.

Mouse says:

The Lord supplies
All our needs.
He gives us berries,
Nuts and seeds.

Let's think…

What kind of things do you need each day? Where do they come from?

Moses led the people out of Egypt and the
Lord went before them in a pillar of cloud by
day and a pillar of fire by night. After seven days'
journey, they reached the shores of the Red Sea.

But back in Egypt, Pharaoh again changed his
mind!

'What have I done?' he cried. 'Why did I let the
Israelite slaves escape? I shall go after them and
make them return to Egypt!'

'Help!' cried the Israelites, when they saw
Pharaoh's army chasing after them. 'What shall
we do? We're trapped between the Egyptians and
the sea!'

Exodus 12:37-42. 14:1-12.

'Don't be frightened!' said the Lord. 'Moses, lift up your stick and hold it out over the sea!'

And as he did, the Lord drove back the sea all night with a strong wind.

'Wow!' cried the children of Israel, when they got up next morning. 'There's a path through the sea!'

And they walked through the sea on dry ground, with walls of water on both sides.

Exodus 14:13-22.

Owl says:
The Lord is full of surprises!

'After them!' cried the captain of Pharaoh's army when he saw the Israelites escaping. And the soldiers rode into the sea with their chariots and drivers.

When all the Israelites were safely on the other side, the Lord said to Moses,

'Hold out your hand over the sea!'

'Right!' said Moses.

Then there was a great crash and the walls of water came tumbling down, covering the Egyptian army. The Israelites were safe at last.

Exodus 14:23-31.

Mole says:

Lord, I don't always know,
What you're going to do,
But help me to learn
To trust in you.

Let's think... What do you do if you get frightened about something?

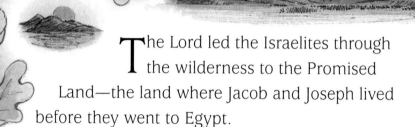

The Lord led the Israelites through the wilderness to the Promised Land—the land where Jacob and Joseph lived before they went to Egypt.

But the people moaned and groaned about anything and everything and were not thankful to Moses or to God for rescuing them from Egypt. So the Lord made them wander in the wilderness for forty years. All through that time, God fed them with a special food, called *manna*."

Exodus 16. Numbers 33.

"Just think," said Mouse, as they arrived at Rabbit's house. "If you hadn't found us, Owl, me and Moley might have been wandering around in Oaktree Wood for forty years!"

Mouse says:

No matter where I wander,
Over land or sea,
There's always someone watching,
Watching over me!

Let's think…Have your parents made any rules for you? Why do you think they make rules?

"There is just one more thing to tell you," said Owl. "While the Israelites were in the wilderness, the Lord gave Moses Ten Commandments carved on stone.

They are the best rules anyone has ever known," said Owl. "And here they are…"

You must have no other gods before me.
Do not make idols to worship.
Do not swear.
You must have one day off a week to rest.
Respect your mum and dad.
Do not murder.
Do not commit adultery.
Do not steal.
Do not tell lies.
Don't be jealous of other people's things.

Exodus 20:1-17.

75

King David

The sun was shining brightly in Oaktree
Wood, and Badger had promised to take his
young friends, Mouse, Mole, Squirrel and Rabbit,
for a swim in the stream. Otter, who lived on the
bank of the stream, was already in the water
when the animals arrived.

"Come on in," he called. "It's lovely!"

So the friends changed into their swimming
suits and jumped into the water.

"Oh, it is lovely!" they squealed, as they
splashed about in the shallows. Badger sat on the
bank in the sunshine, reading his book. At last,
the tired animals climbed out of the stream and
shook the water from their fur. It went all over
Badger!

"Hey!" he laughed. "Mind my book!"

"Sorry, Badger," said Mouse. "What are you
reading?"

"Oh, just a story," said Badger.

"Tell it us, Badger, please!" said Mouse.

"Oh, all right," said Badger.

"It all began after the Israelites had settled in Canaan—The Promised Land," said Badger.

"'We want a king!' the people told Samuel the Prophet. 'We want a king over us who will fight our battles and lead us out to war, like the other countries around us!'

1 Samuel:8:4-5.

Say a prayer with Rabbit:

Lord, your way is so much better
Than any other way,
So help us not to want the things
That make us go astray.

Let's think…

Do we want to be like the other people around us?

Samuel didn't like the idea at all. 'A king will take your sons and daughters and make them serve in his army and work in his fields,' he said. 'And he will make you pay heavy taxes!'

But the people paid no attention to Samuel.

So the Lord told Samuel to anoint a tall, handsome young man named Saul, to be the first king of Israel.

1 Samuel 8:6-22. 9:15-17.

Say a prayer with Squirrel:
Lord, teach me to listen,
When others explain,
About ways that will bring,
Unhappiness and pain.

Let's think…
Paul tells us to "always be joyful." 1 Thes. 5:16

79

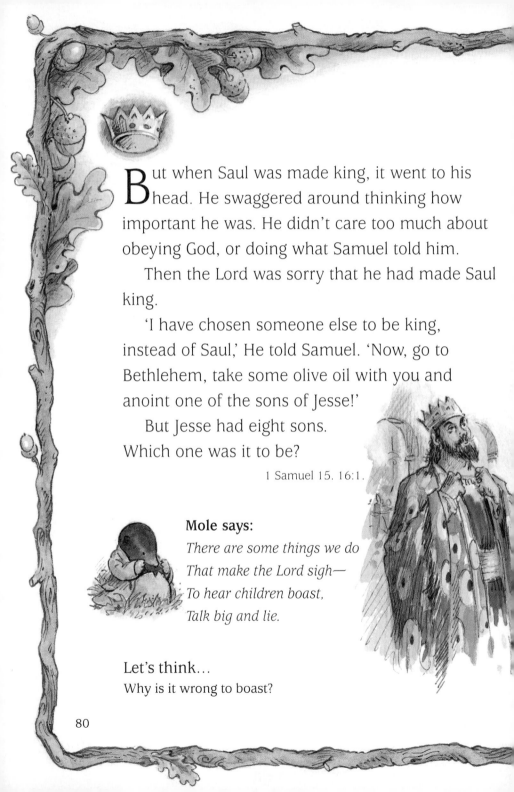

But when Saul was made king, it went to his head. He swaggered around thinking how important he was. He didn't care too much about obeying God, or doing what Samuel told him.

Then the Lord was sorry that he had made Saul king.

'I have chosen someone else to be king, instead of Saul,' He told Samuel. 'Now, go to Bethlehem, take some olive oil with you and anoint one of the sons of Jesse!'

But Jesse had eight sons.
Which one was it to be?

1 Samuel 15. 16:1.

Mole says:
There are some things we do
That make the Lord sigh—
To hear children boast,
Talk big and lie.

Let's think…
Why is it wrong to boast?

When Samuel saw Eliab, Jesse's oldest son, he thought,

'This must be the man!'

'No! It isn't him!' said the Lord. 'Pay no attention to how tall and handsome he is, for I do not judge as man judges. Man looks at what he can see on the outside, but I look at the heart— what people are like on the inside!'

1 Samuel 16:6-7.

Mouse says:

The Lord chooses those
Who are gentle and kind,
To do His work
For all humankind.

Let's think…

God knows what is in your heart.

Jesse brought seven of his sons before Samuel, but God chose none of them.

'No!' said Samuel. 'It is not any of these. Haven't you got any more sons anywhere?'

'Yes, there is the youngest,' said Jesse. 'But he is out taking care of the sheep.'

'Fetch him!' said Samuel.

1 Samuel 16:8-11.

David's most famous song:

The Lord is my shepherd;
I shall not want.
He makes me to lie down in green pastures;

Badger says:

David wrote many songs. We can read them in the book of Psalms.

So Jesse sent for his youngest son, David, who was a shepherd boy. David was also a musician, he played the harp and wrote and sang songs. He was a fine looking boy with rosy cheeks and sparkling eyes.

'This is the one!' the Lord told Samuel.

And so, to the astonishment of his brothers, Samuel poured the oil over David's head, and anointed him as the next King of Israel!

1 Samuel 16:12-13.

David's song continued:
He leads me beside the still waters.
He restores my soul;
He leads me in the paths of righteousness
For His name's sake.   Psalm 23

Mouse says:
The Lord called David 'a man after His own heart.' (1Sam. 13:14)

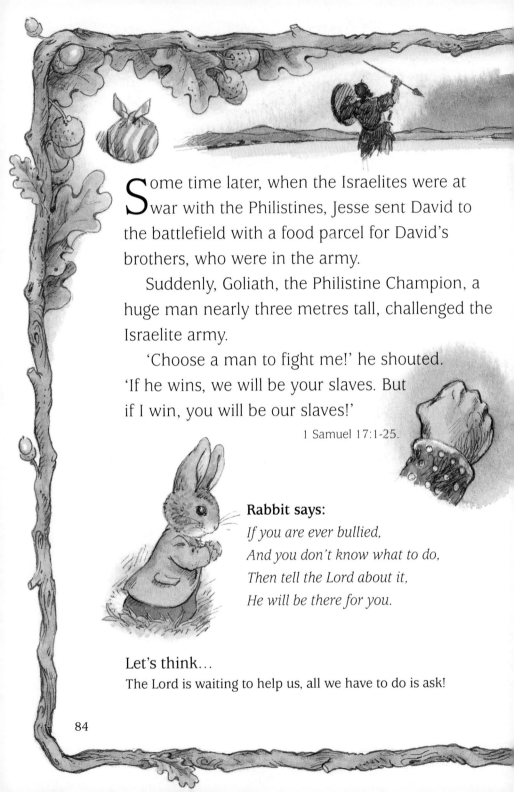

Some time later, when the Israelites were at war with the Philistines, Jesse sent David to the battlefield with a food parcel for David's brothers, who were in the army.

Suddenly, Goliath, the Philistine Champion, a huge man nearly three metres tall, challenged the Israelite army.

'Choose a man to fight me!' he shouted. 'If he wins, we will be your slaves. But if I win, you will be our slaves!'

1 Samuel 17:1-25.

Rabbit says:
If you are ever bullied,
And you don't know what to do,
Then tell the Lord about it,
He will be there for you.

Let's think…
The Lord is waiting to help us, all we have to do is ask!

King Saul and his men were terrified.

'What are we going to do?' they cried.

'No one is brave enough to fight Goliath!'

But David was not frightened.

'Who does this heathen Philistine think he is,' he cried, 'that he defies the armies of the living God?'

1 Samuel 17:26-30.

Squirrel says:

Do not worry
What people say and do,
For the Lord will take
Good care of you.

Let's think…

With the Lord beside us we are never alone.

When King Saul heard what David was saying, he sent for him.

'No need to worry about Goliath,' David said. 'I will fight him!'

'Don't be ridiculous!' said Saul. 'You're only a boy!'

'I may be young,' said David, 'but I look after my father's sheep, and if a wild animal tries to steal a lamb, I go after it and rescue the lamb. Then if the animal turns on me, I kill it! I have killed lions and bears! And the Lord, who has saved me from these wild animals, will save me from this Philistine, too!'

1 Samuel 17:31-37

Mole says:
The God who helps me
Day by day,
I promise truly
To obey.

Let's think... The Lord can save us, too. What do you think He saves us from?

86

'All right,' said Saul. 'Go and fight Goliath, and may the Lord be with you! But first, you must wear my armor to protect you.' And he put his helmet on David's head and helped him into his coat of mail.

Then David strapped Saul's sword over the armor and tried to walk. But he couldn't!

1 Samuel 17:37-39.

Rabbit says:

*God's armor is ready
For His children to wear.
It is made with His love,
His word, and prayer.*

Let's think…
What do you think God's armor protects us from?

'I can't fight with this on,' said David. 'I'm not used to it!' So he took it all off again.

Then, just taking his slingshot, he chose five smooth stones from the stream and went out to meet Goliath. When the Philistine giant saw David running towards him, he laughed.

'Am I a dog!' he shouted, 'that you come to me with sticks and stones?' And he cursed David in the name of his gods.

1 Samuel 17:39-44.

Mouse says:
Sticks and stones
May break my bones
But names will never hurt me!

Let's think…
Sometimes, though, when people call us names it does hurt— it hurts our feelings. What should we do when this happens?

'You come to me with a sword and a spear and a javelin!' cried David. 'But I come to you in the name of the Lord Almighty—God of the armies of Israel, whom you have defied! This day the Lord will deliver you into my hand, then all the earth will know that there is a God in Israel!'

1 Samuel 17:45-47.

Say a prayer with Squirrel:
Lord, help me believe,
With all my might,
That your word is true,
And your way, right.

Let's think…
Why do you think David was so sure that God would help him?

T hen, running towards Goliath, David took one of the stones from his bag and put it in his sling. He slung the sling around his head and let the stone fly. WHOOSH! It hit Goliath and sank into his forehead. The great Philistine fell flat on his face to the ground. Then David ran and took the giant's sword out of its sheath and cut off his head!

1 Samuel 17:48-51.

Mole says:
Giant worries,
Giant fears,
Giant problems disappear
When the Lord is standing near.

Let's think…
The Lord will give us courage if we ask Him.

'Hooray!' shouted the Israelite soldiers.

'Help!' cried the Philistines, when they saw their champion was dead. 'Let's get out of here!' and they ran away as fast as they could. The Israelites ran after them and chased them back to their own land.

David picked up Goliath's head and took it to Jerusalem.

1 Samuel 17:51-54.

Badger says:
Chase away your troubles,
Chase away your cares,
For the Lord will answer
All your heartfelt prayers.

Let's think…
Everyone has difficulties sometimes, but difficulties can be worked out.

After that, Saul made David an officer in his army. David became a great soldier and was successful on all his missions. He was so popular with the people, that the women sang songs about him. This made Saul so jealous, he tried to kill David. But with the help of his friend, Jonathan, David escaped to safety in the hills.   1 Samuel 18-20.

Say a prayer with Mouse:
Thank you, dear Lord,
For making things right,
For those who love you,
And trust in your might.

Let's think…
Would you like to be popular?

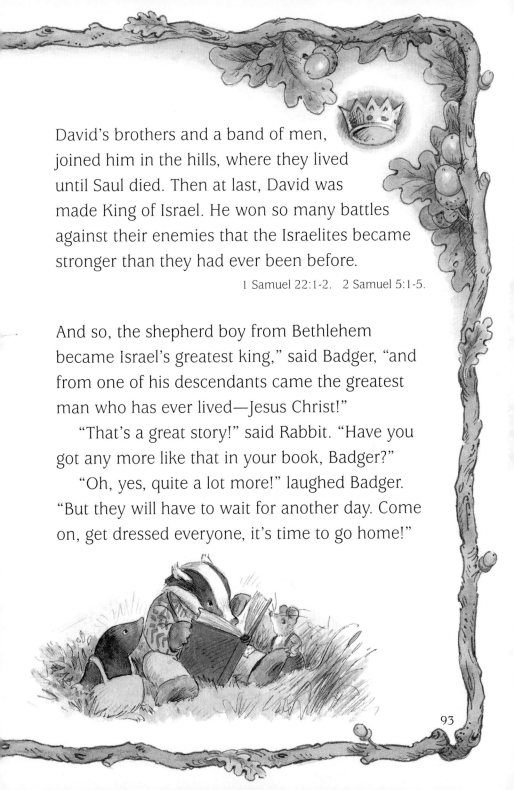

David's brothers and a band of men, joined him in the hills, where they lived until Saul died. Then at last, David was made King of Israel. He won so many battles against their enemies that the Israelites became stronger than they had ever been before.

1 Samuel 22:1-2. 2 Samuel 5:1-5.

And so, the shepherd boy from Bethlehem became Israel's greatest king," said Badger, "and from one of his descendants came the greatest man who has ever lived—Jesus Christ!"

"That's a great story!" said Rabbit. "Have you got any more like that in your book, Badger?"

"Oh, yes, quite a lot more!" laughed Badger. "But they will have to wait for another day. Come on, get dressed everyone, it's time to go home!"

Jonah

A howling wind swept through the trees in Oaktree Wood making the boughs sway and creak.

Suddenly, there was a flash of lightning and the great branch on which Squirrel had built her home, cracked and broke. Squirrel leapt to safety, but her home crashed to the ground in pieces. She spent the rest of the night sheltering in Badger's house.

"Never mind," said Badger, "in the morning we will build you a new home!"

Rabbit, Mouse and Mole were sheltering from the storm in Badger's house, too. They didn't like the thunder. Badger made them all a cup of hot cocoa.

"Well now," he said, "this storm reminds me of a story I know."

"Oh, tell it to us, Badger, please," said Squirrel. "Perhaps it will help to cheer me up!"

"It all began in the city of Nineveh, in Assyria," said Badger.

"'The people of Nineveh are so wicked,' said the Lord. 'I don't like to see them being so bad to one another. I must do something about it!'

Squirrel says:

The Lord weeps
When people are bad,
Their wicked ways
Make Him sad.

Let's think…

When people do bad things, it makes everyone sad.

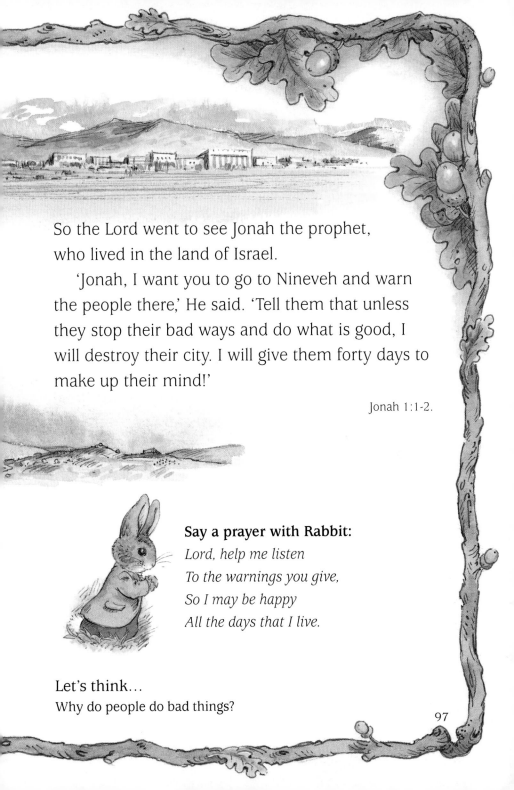

So the Lord went to see Jonah the prophet, who lived in the land of Israel.

'Jonah, I want you to go to Nineveh and warn the people there,' He said. 'Tell them that unless they stop their bad ways and do what is good, I will destroy their city. I will give them forty days to make up their mind!'

Jonah 1:1-2.

Say a prayer with Rabbit:
*Lord, help me listen
To the warnings you give,
So I may be happy
All the days that I live.*

Let's think...
Why do people do bad things?

97

B ut Jonah didn't like this idea at all.
'I hate the Assyrians!' he thought. 'They're our worst enemies! Why should the Lord worry about them? Why doesn't He just zap them—that's what I would do! But no! He's going to give them a chance to repent. Well, I'm not going to be the one to warn them! I'm getting out of here!'

Jonah 4:1-3.

Mole says:

The Lord loves all the children,
All the children of the world,
Red and yellow, black and white,
All are precious in His sight.

Let's think…
Do we give others a chance to say sorry?

So Jonah loaded his donkey
and rode as fast as he could to the
seaside town of Joppa. There he saw a
boat ready to set sail for Spain.

'Can I sail with you to Spain, please?' Jonah
asked the captain.

'If you're quick,' replied the captain. 'We're
about to pull anchor!'

So Jonah paid his fare money and hurried on
board.

Jonah 1:3.

Say a prayer with Mouse:
*Lord, let me not rush away from doing
the things I should.*

Everything was fine at first, the sky was blue and the sun sparkled on the water.

'Ah, this is the life!' said Jonah, as he settled down for a good sleep below deck. 'The Lord will never find me out here, in the middle of the sea!'

Jonah 1:3.

Badger says:
Lord, let me not try to hide from you.

Let's think…
Do you think the Lord can see you now?

But Oh, dear! The Lord knew exactly where Jonah was, and He wasn't very pleased about it. So He sent a great wind on the sea, which churned up the waves.

The sailors tried hard to keep the boat on course. But it was no good. The sea was too rough and the boat was bobbing about out of control.

'Haul down the sails,' ordered the captain. 'We will wait till this gale dies down!'

Jonah 1:4.

Squirrel says:

The Lord will show the way,
No matter what we do or say.

Let's think...

Do you think the Lord's way is for our own good?

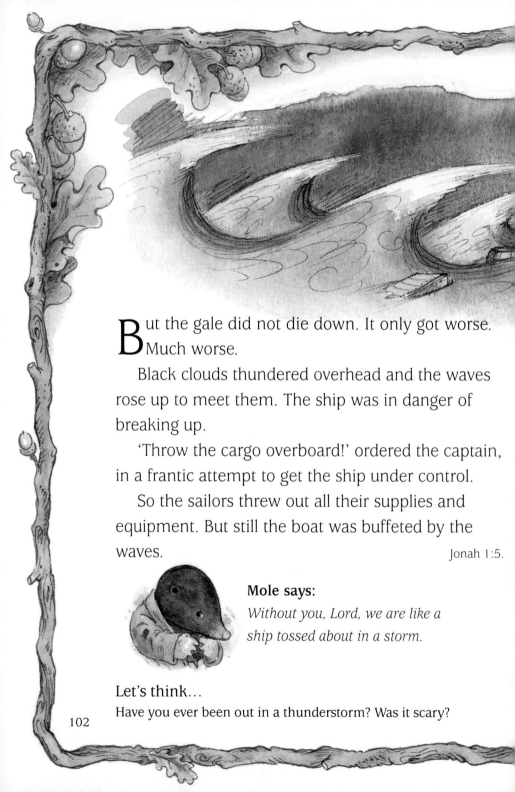

But the gale did not die down. It only got worse. Much worse.

Black clouds thundered overhead and the waves rose up to meet them. The ship was in danger of breaking up.

'Throw the cargo overboard!' ordered the captain, in a frantic attempt to get the ship under control.

So the sailors threw out all their supplies and equipment. But still the boat was buffeted by the waves.

Jonah 1:5.

Mole says:

Without you, Lord, we are like a ship tossed about in a storm.

Let's think...

Have you ever been out in a thunderstorm? Was it scary?

102

Then the sailors began to pray to their gods.
But nothing happened. The sky grew even darker
and waves higher.

'Where's Jonah?' asked the captain. 'He ought to
be praying to *his* God.'

The captain found Jonah fast asleep below deck.

'Wake up!' he cried. 'Don't you know we're in
terrible danger? Get up and pray to your God!
Maybe he will save us!'

Jonah 1:5-6.

Squirrel says:

Whenever you're in trouble,
You must without delay,
Put your hands together,
And PRAY! PRAY! PRAY!

Let's think…
What kind of things can we pray to God about?

'Let's find out who's to blame for getting us into this danger!' said one of the sailors. So they drew lots and Jonah's name came up.

'What have you done?' they asked him.

'I'm running away from the Lord,' said Jonah. 'The one who made the land and the sea and everything there is!'

When the sailors heard this they were terrified.

Jonah 1:7-10.

Rabbit says:

Lord, sometimes we run
From the way you taught,
'cause we don't want to do
The things we ought.

Let's see…

Do you think it's possible to run away from the Lord?

'What shall we do?' they asked him.
'Throw me overboard!' said Jonah.
'Then the storm will stop.'
'What!' they cried. 'We can't do that!' So
they tried hard to row for shore. But they could
not reach it. The wind was against them.
    Then at last, they cried out to the Lord,
    'O Lord, don't punish us for this!' And they
picked Jonah up and threw him into the sea!

Jonah 1:11-15.

Say a prayer with Mole:
*You are beneath, Lord,
And you are above,
Wherever we go,
We will find your love.*

Let's see…
Do you think Jonah was beginning to wish he had not
disobeyed the Lord?

Immediately, the storm stopped and the sea became calm.

'Wow!' said one of the sailors. 'That's some God that Jonah worships!'

'Yea,' said another, 'He must be so powerful!'

'O Lord God of the land and sea and everything there is,' prayed the sailors. 'Thank you for saving us. From now on, we will only worship you!'

Jonah 1:15-16.

Mouse says:

The Lord has all power
Over land and sea,
So mighty and strong
And yet He loves me!

Let's think…
We can be sure that the Great One loves every one of us.

Meanwhile, Jonah fell down and
down to the bottom of the sea.

Then suddenly, a great big fish appeared.

'Go and rescue Jonah,' God told the fish.
'And keep him safe inside you!'

So the big fish opened its huge mouth and
swallowed Jonah whole!

107 Jonah 1:17.

Rabbit says:

Just when you think that all is lost,
And you don't know what to do,
The Lord will come—He won't delay,
He'll come to rescue you.

107

Then, from deep inside the fish's tummy, Jonah prayed to the Lord.

'I sank down beneath the waves to the bottom of the sea, but you did not let me die. You sent your fish to rescue me. Thank you, Lord. Please forgive me for running away. I am truly sorry.'

Jonah 2:1-9.

Badger says:

The Great One forgives,
I know it is true,
All the bad things we say
And the wrong things we do.

Let's think…

No matter where you are, God hears your prayers.

After three days and nights, the Lord said to the fish,
'Swim to the shore and spit up Jonah onto the
beach.'

So the big fish swam into the shallows, opened its
huge mouth once more, and WHOOSH! Jonah was
free at last!

Jonah 2:10.

Mole says:

When we trust in the Lord,
Everything turns out right in the end.

Let's see…What do you think Jonah looked like after being
inside the fish for three days and three nights?

109

'Now,' said the Lord again, when Jonah had recovered from his ride in the fish. 'Go to Nineveh and give the people my message!'

And this time, Jonah went.

'In forty days Nineveh will be destroyed!' Jonah told the people.

'Oh, dear!' they cried. 'What must we do?'

'You must stop being bad and do what is good!' Jonah told them.

Jonah 3:1-5.

"The Lord has a message for all of us," said Badger:

'This is what I want you to do,' says the Lord.

'Love one another, as I have loved you.'

John 15:12.

Let's think…When we love the Lord, it is easy to love others.

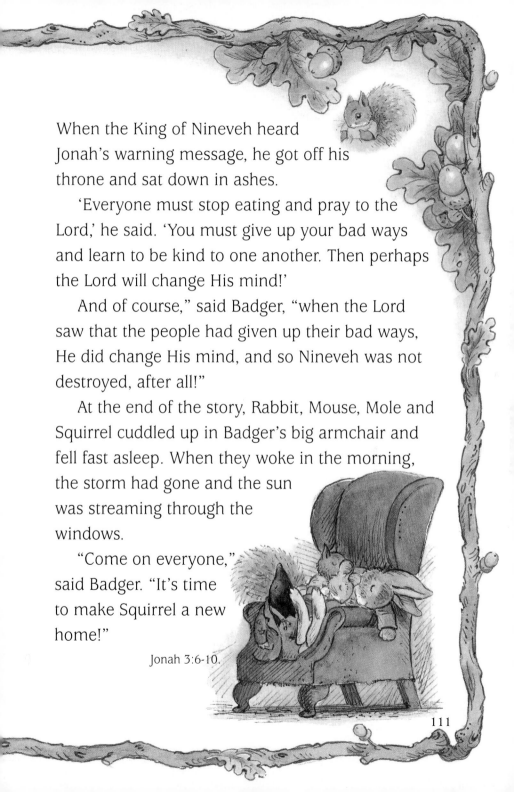

When the King of Nineveh heard
Jonah's warning message, he got off his
throne and sat down in ashes.

'Everyone must stop eating and pray to the
Lord,' he said. 'You must give up your bad ways
and learn to be kind to one another. Then perhaps
the Lord will change His mind!'

And of course," said Badger, "when the Lord
saw that the people had given up their bad ways,
He did change His mind, and so Nineveh was not
destroyed, after all!"

At the end of the story, Rabbit, Mouse, Mole and
Squirrel cuddled up in Badger's big armchair and
fell fast asleep. When they woke in the morning,
the storm had gone and the sun
was streaming through the
windows.

"Come on everyone,"
said Badger. "It's time
to make Squirrel a new
home!"

Jonah 3:6-10.

Daniel

Mouse and Mole were gathering blackberries in Oaktree Wood, when suddenly, they caught sight of a stray fox hiding behind one of the oak trees. He was watching them closely.

"Do you think he's hungry?" said Mouse.

"Probably," said Mole. "Badger's house is not far off. Let's make for that as fast as we can."

They ran, panting and trembling until at last they reached Badger's house. They threw open the door and tumbled inside.

"Sorry, Badger, for rushing in uninvited," cried Mouse. "But there's a big fox out there!"

"Is there now!" said Badger,
and he strode out waving a big stick
and chased the strange fox away. Then
he made his little friends a cup of rosehip
tea to calm their nerves.

"We were so frightened!" said Mouse.

"Well, I think you were very brave," said Badger.
"Look, sit for awhile in the big armchair and I will
read you a story. It's about Daniel. He was very
brave, too."

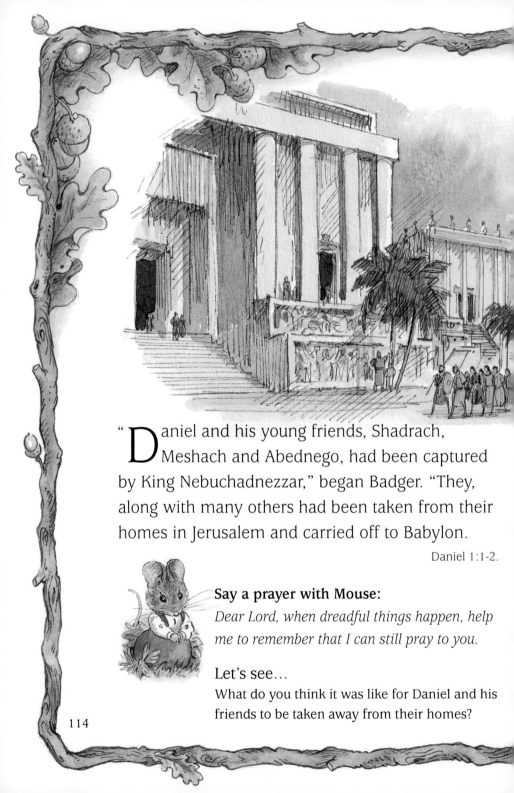

"Daniel and his young friends, Shadrach, Meshach and Abednego, had been captured by King Nebuchadnezzar," began Badger. "They, along with many others had been taken from their homes in Jerusalem and carried off to Babylon.

Daniel 1:1-2.

Say a prayer with Mouse:
Dear Lord, when dreadful things happen, help me to remember that I can still pray to you.

Let's see…
What do you think it was like for Daniel and his friends to be taken away from their homes?

King Nebuchadnezzar put
Ashpenaz, his chief official, in charge
of the captives.

'I need some handsome and intelligent
young men to work in the palace,' the king told
him. 'Choose some from these captives. And make
sure they come from royal or noble families.'

Daniel 1:3-4

Say a prayer with Mole:
*No matter where I am, Lord,
help me to remember that you
are beside me.*

Let's think…
If we love the Lord, then we will never, ever be alone.

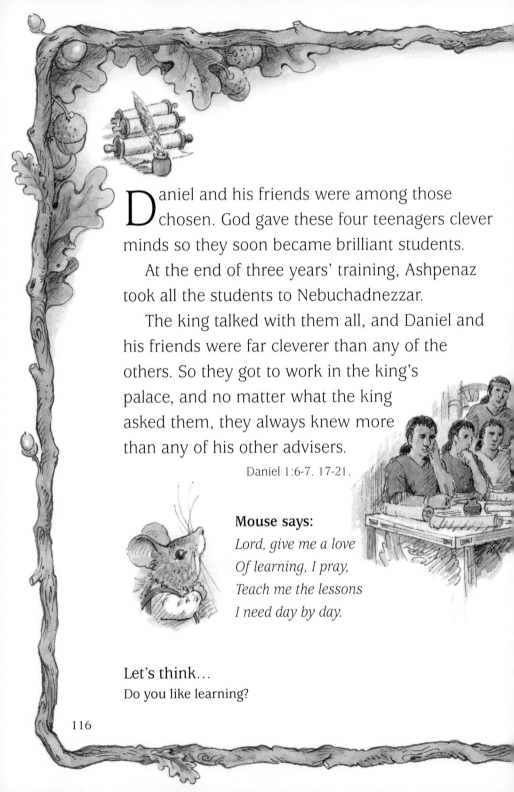

D aniel and his friends were among those chosen. God gave these four teenagers clever minds so they soon became brilliant students.

At the end of three years' training, Ashpenaz took all the students to Nebuchadnezzar.

The king talked with them all, and Daniel and his friends were far cleverer than any of the others. So they got to work in the king's palace, and no matter what the king asked them, they always knew more than any of his other advisers.

Daniel 1:6-7. 17-21.

Mouse says:

*Lord, give me a love
Of learning, I pray,
Teach me the lessons
I need day by day.*

Let's think…
Do you like learning?

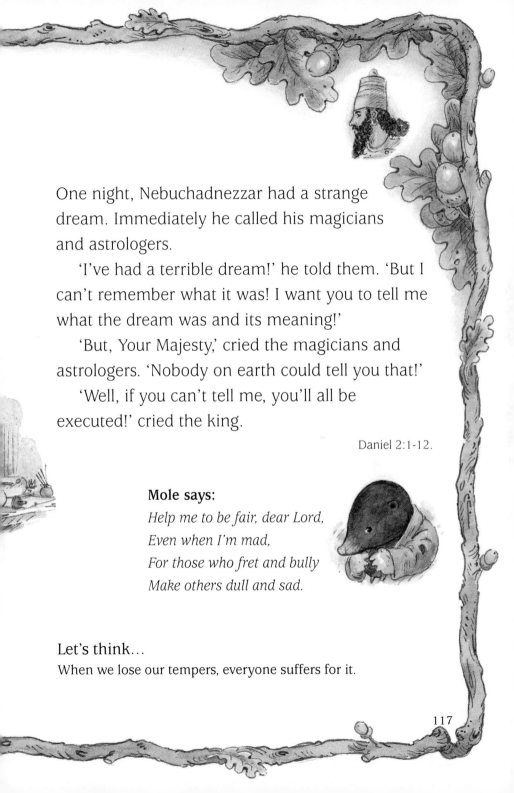

One night, Nebuchadnezzar had a strange dream. Immediately he called his magicians and astrologers.

'I've had a terrible dream!' he told them. 'But I can't remember what it was! I want you to tell me what the dream was and its meaning!'

'But, Your Majesty,' cried the magicians and astrologers. 'Nobody on earth could tell you that!'

'Well, if you can't tell me, you'll all be executed!' cried the king.

Daniel 2:1-12.

Mole says:

Help me to be fair, dear Lord,
Even when I'm mad,
For those who fret and bully
Make others dull and sad.

Let's think…
When we lose our tempers, everyone suffers for it.

117

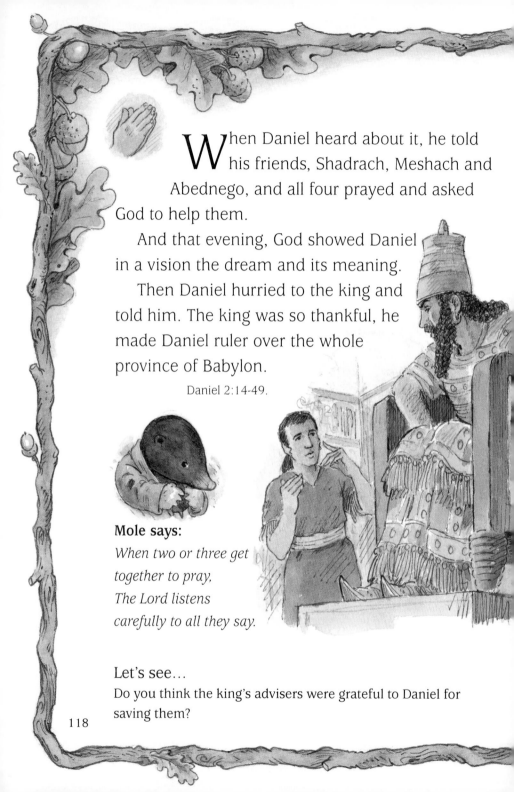

When Daniel heard about it, he told his friends, Shadrach, Meshach and Abednego, and all four prayed and asked God to help them.

And that evening, God showed Daniel in a vision the dream and its meaning.

Then Daniel hurried to the king and told him. The king was so thankful, he made Daniel ruler over the whole province of Babylon.

Daniel 2:14-49.

Mole says:

When two or three get together to pray,
The Lord listens
carefully to all they say.

Let's see…

Do you think the king's advisers were grateful to Daniel for saving them?

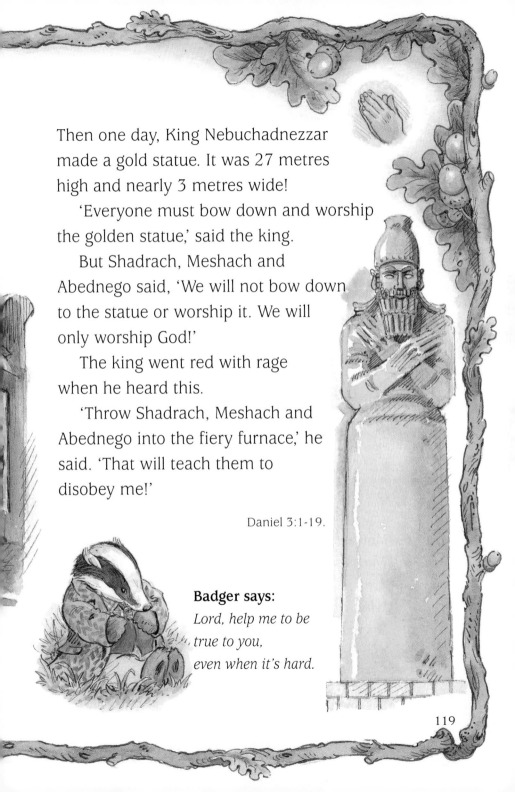

Then one day, King Nebuchadnezzar made a gold statue. It was 27 metres high and nearly 3 metres wide!

'Everyone must bow down and worship the golden statue,' said the king.

But Shadrach, Meshach and Abednego said, 'We will not bow down to the statue or worship it. We will only worship God!'

The king went red with rage when he heard this.

'Throw Shadrach, Meshach and Abednego into the fiery furnace,' he said. 'That will teach them to disobey me!'

Daniel 3:1-19.

Badger says:
Lord, help me to be true to you, even when it's hard.

119

So the guards tied up Shadrach, Meshach and Abednego and threw them into the heart of the blazing furnace!

Suddenly, Nebuchadnezzar cried out in amazement. 'Didn't we tie up three men and throw them into the furnace?'

'Yes, we did!' said the guards.

'Then why can I see four men walking about in the flames? he cried. 'And one of them looks like an angel!'

Daniel 3:20-25

Mouse says:
Things begin to happen,
Lord,
When we trust in you,
For you have all the power
And the glory, too.

Let's see…Have you ever thought about God's power?

'Shadrach, Meshach and Abednego, followers of the true God,' called Nebuchadnezzar. 'Come out!'

So they came out, and the fire had not harmed a hair on their head! They did not even smell of smoke!

'Praise the God of Shadrach, Meshach and Abednego, who sent His angel to rescue them from the fiery furnace,' said the king. 'They risked their lives because of their love for their God. Now I command that everyone in every nation respect their God.

Daniel 3:26-30.

Mole says:
Great God, thank you for saving Shadrach, Meshach and Abednego from the fiery furnace.

121

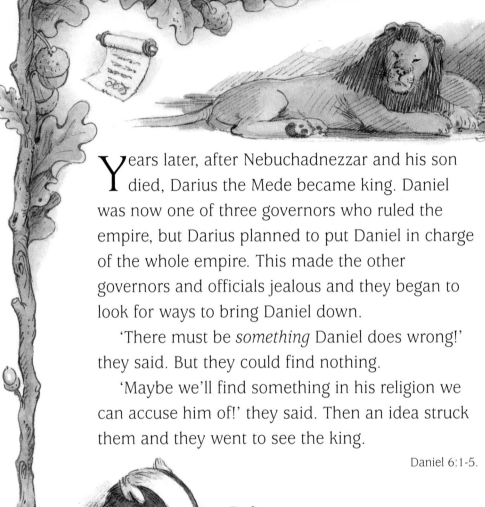

Years later, after Nebuchadnezzar and his son died, Darius the Mede became king. Daniel was now one of three governors who ruled the empire, but Darius planned to put Daniel in charge of the whole empire. This made the other governors and officials jealous and they began to look for ways to bring Daniel down.

'There must be *something* Daniel does wrong!' they said. But they could find nothing.

'Maybe we'll find something in his religion we can accuse him of!' they said. Then an idea struck them and they went to see the king.

Daniel 6:1-5.

Badger says:
Evil thoughts bring evil deeds,
And evil deeds bring death!

Let's think…
If we fill our minds up with good and lovely thoughts, there won't be any space left for bad.

'O king, live for ever!' they said. 'Your officials and governors have agreed that Your Majesty should give orders that for thirty days no one is allowed to ask anything of any God or man except from Your Majesty. Anyone who disobeys this order is to be thrown into the lions' den!'

So King Darius signed the order. It was a law of the Medes and Persians, which could not be broken.

Daniel 6:6-9.

Say a prayer with Mouse:
Teach me to be honest, Lord,
In all I say and do,
For you hate all lies and falsehood
But love what's right and true.

Let's think…
Do you wonder why King Darius signed the order?

123

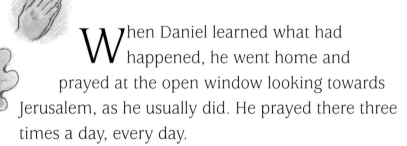

When Daniel learned what had happened, he went home and prayed at the open window looking towards Jerusalem, as he usually did. He prayed there three times a day, every day.

The wicked governors were waiting for him.

'Look!' they cried, when they saw Daniel at the window. 'Daniel is praying to his God. Let's go and tell the king!'

The king was mad when he realized he had been tricked into setting a trap for Daniel. He tried hard to find a way to rescue him. But he could not. For the law of the Medes and Persians could not be broken.

Daniel 6:10-15.

Say a prayer with Mole:
Give me courage, Lord,
To stand up for you,
Even when others
Make fun when I do.

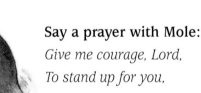

Let's see…
Do you think Daniel was brave, praying to God when he did?

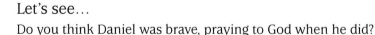

So Daniel was arrested and thrown into the den of lions.

'May your God, whom you pray to every day, rescue you,' said the king.

A great stone was rolled over the entrance to the den and then the king returned to the palace. He could not sleep that night and he refused to eat or be entertained.

Daniel 6:16-18.

When Badger is in trouble, he says:
Dear Lord Comforter,
Rescue me,
Take away my troubles,
Set me free!

Let's see…
Do you think Daniel knew that the Lord would rescue him?

125

The next morning, the king rushed to the lions' den and called out, 'Daniel, O Daniel, are you still alive? Has the God that you serve so loyally been able to save you from the lions?'

'Yes!' cried out Daniel. 'I am alive and well! The dear God that I serve sent His angel to shut the mouths of the lions so they could not hurt me!'

Daniel 6:19-22.

Mouse says:

You are so full, Lord,
Of goodness and might,
I think about you
Both day and night.

Let's see…
Have you ever thought about God's goodness?

The king wept for joy and ordered that Daniel be released immediately.

Then he ordered that the wicked governors and officials who had plotted against Daniel, be arrested and thrown into the den of lions!

Daniel 6:23-24.

Say a prayer with Mole:
Dear Great One, you love what is true,
Help us little ones to love it too.

Let's think…
It is best to stand up for what is right.

127

After that, King Darius sent a letter to all the people in all the nations in his empire.

'Greetings!

I command that everyone in my kingdom must fear and respect the God of Daniel.

For He is a living God and He lives forever. His Kingdom will never be destroyed. He rescues and saves and does wonderful things. And He rescued Daniel from the lions!'"

Daniel 6:25-28.

Say a prayer with Badger:
Give us eyes to see, dear Lord,
The wonder of your power.
You formed the trees in Oaktree Wood,
Each plant and shady bower,
You care for every tiny bird
And clothe each woodland flower.

Let's think...
Let us never grow tired of wondering.

"It just goes to show," said Mole, when Badger came to the end of the story, "how important it is to be on the right side!"

"Why—what do you mean?" asked Mouse.

"Well—the bad governors weren't on the side of the Great One—and look what happened to them!" said Mole.

"That's true," said Badger. "If we are on the right side, then in the end, everything will turn out right, just like it did for Daniel!"

Then Badger walked with Mouse and Mole through the wood, back to their own little homes, just in case they should meet the fox again. But they needn't have worried. No stray fox would dare come into the wood while Badger was around.

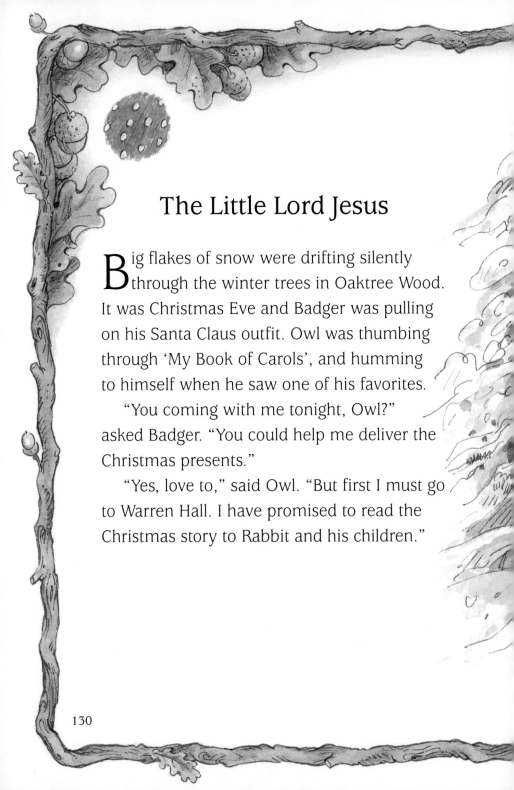

The Little Lord Jesus

Big flakes of snow were drifting silently through the winter trees in Oaktree Wood. It was Christmas Eve and Badger was pulling on his Santa Claus outfit. Owl was thumbing through 'My Book of Carols', and humming to himself when he saw one of his favorites.

"You coming with me tonight, Owl?" asked Badger. "You could help me deliver the Christmas presents."

"Yes, love to," said Owl. "But first I must go to Warren Hall. I have promised to read the Christmas story to Rabbit and his children."

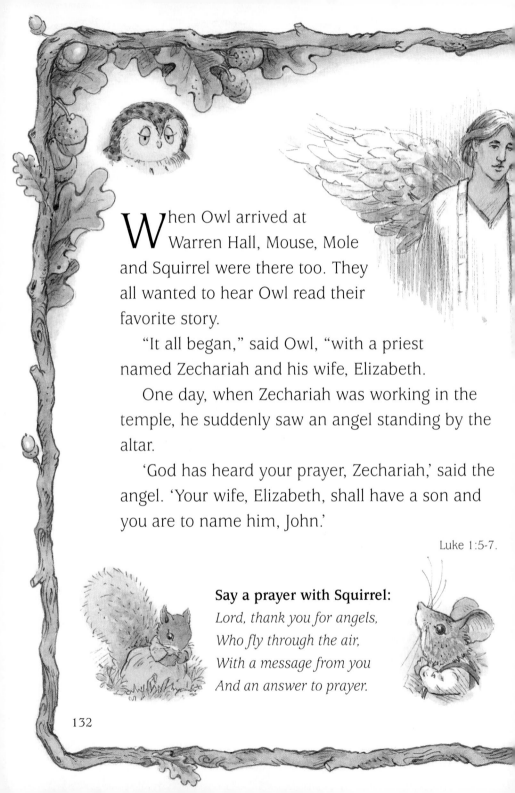

When Owl arrived at Warren Hall, Mouse, Mole and Squirrel were there too. They all wanted to hear Owl read their favorite story.

"It all began," said Owl, "with a priest named Zechariah and his wife, Elizabeth.

One day, when Zechariah was working in the temple, he suddenly saw an angel standing by the altar.

'God has heard your prayer, Zechariah,' said the angel. 'Your wife, Elizabeth, shall have a son and you are to name him, John.'

Luke 1:5-7.

Say a prayer with Squirrel:
Lord, thank you for angels,
Who fly through the air,
With a message from you
And an answer to prayer.

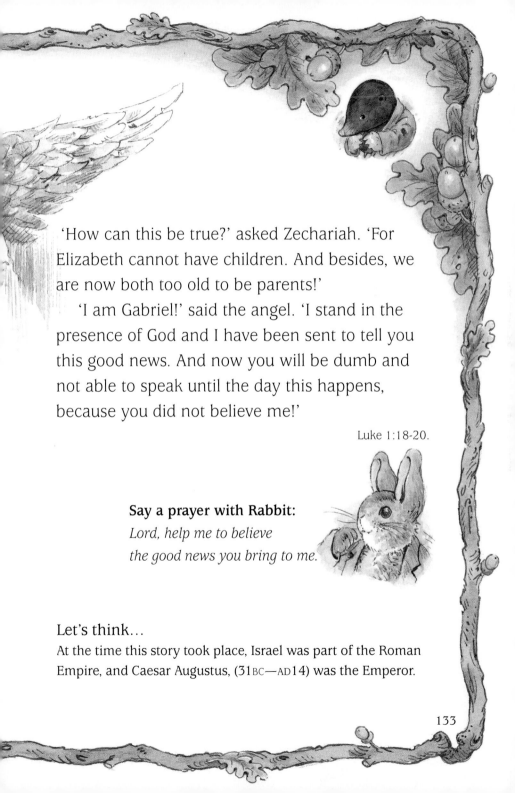

'How can this be true?' asked Zechariah. 'For Elizabeth cannot have children. And besides, we are now both too old to be parents!'

'I am Gabriel!' said the angel. 'I stand in the presence of God and I have been sent to tell you this good news. And now you will be dumb and not able to speak until the day this happens, because you did not believe me!'

Luke 1:18-20.

Say a prayer with Rabbit:
Lord, help me to believe
the good news you bring to me.

Let's think...
At the time this story took place, Israel was part of the Roman Empire, and Caesar Augustus, (31BC—AD14) was the Emperor.

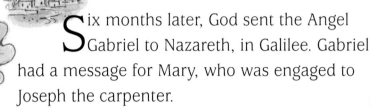

Six months later, God sent the Angel Gabriel to Nazareth, in Galilee. Gabriel had a message for Mary, who was engaged to Joseph the carpenter.

'Greetings, O chosen one,' said Gabriel. 'The Lord is with you.'

Mary was frightened. What did the angel want with her?

'God wants you to be the mother of a son,' said Gabriel. 'He will be great and will rule over Israel for ever. His kingdom will never end.'

'But how can I have a baby?' asked Mary. 'I do not have a husband.'

'The Holy Spirit will come upon you,' said the angel, 'for the child will be the Son of God!'

Luke 1:26-38.

Say a prayer with Mouse:
Thank you for choosing, Lord,
A girl so sweet—
An ordinary girl
You could meet in the street.

Mary wanted to share her exciting
news with her cousin, Elizabeth. So she
set off to visit her. When Elizabeth heard
Mary come into the house, the baby inside her
leapt for joy.

'Blessed are you among women,' cried Elizabeth.
'And blessed is the child in your womb! But
why am I so honored that the mother of
my Lord should visit me?'

Luke 1:39-45.

Say a prayer with Mole:
*When something good happens for others and they
want to share it, help me, Lord, to be happy too.*

Let's think…
When Elizabeth spoke to Mary she was filled with the Holy
Spirit. Do you know what the Holy Spirit is?

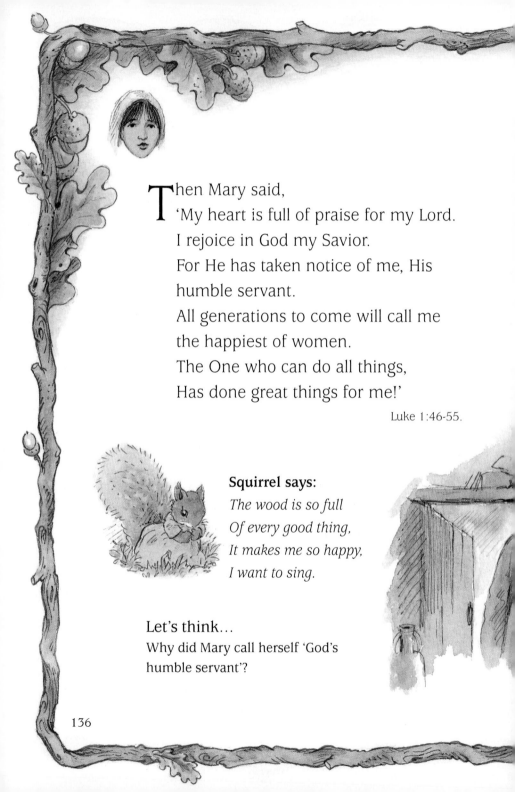

Then Mary said,
'My heart is full of praise for my Lord.
I rejoice in God my Savior.
For He has taken notice of me, His humble servant.
All generations to come will call me the happiest of women.
The One who can do all things,
Has done great things for me!'

Luke 1:46-55.

Squirrel says:
The wood is so full
Of every good thing,
It makes me so happy,
I want to sing.

Let's think…
Why did Mary call herself 'God's humble servant'?

136

Mary stayed with Elizabeth for three months, and then she went back home.

When the time came for Elizabeth to have her baby, she gave birth to a son. Her family wanted to call him Zechariah, after his father, but Elizabeth said, 'No! He is to be called, John!'

So they made signs to his father, to find out what he would like to name the child.

And Zechariah wrote, 'His name is John.'

Immediately, Zechariah was able to speak again and he started praising God.

Luke 1:56-66.

Owl says:

When we obey God,
And don't argue or fight,
Things will get better,
They'll turn out all right!

Let's think…
Do you know who chose your name?

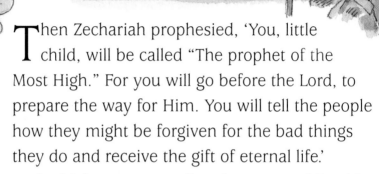

Then Zechariah prophesied, 'You, little child, will be called "The prophet of the Most High." For you will go before the Lord, to prepare the way for Him. You will tell the people how they might be forgiven for the bad things they do and receive the gift of eternal life.'

And John grew up tall and strong and lived in the desert until it was time for him to teach the people.

Luke 1:67-80.

Mouse says:

There's a gift that is on offer,
Which comes from heaven above,
It waits for you to claim it,
Its only cost is love.

Let's see…
A prophet is someone who tells about things that are to come.

Meanwhile, back in Nazareth, Joseph the carpenter had discovered that Mary was going to have a baby.

'Mary must be seeing another man,' he thought. 'I won't be able to marry her now.'

But that night, an angel appeared to him in a dream.

'Joseph, don't be frightened to take Mary as your wife,' said the angel. 'For the child growing inside her is from God. She will have a Son, and you are to name Him "Jesus" because He will save His people from their sins.'

Matthew 1:18-21.

Rabbit says:
Lord, thank you that Joseph believed the angel.

Let's think...
Jesus means 'God saves.'

When Joseph woke up, he married Mary, as the angel had told him to do. Soon after, Caesar Augustus ordered that the people of the Roman Empire should be counted. All the people had to return to the town of their ancestors to be registered.

Mary and Joseph were descendants of King David, so they had to travel to Bethlehem in Judea, where David was born.

When they reached Bethlehem, the time came for Mary's baby to be born.

Matthew 1:24. Luke 2:1-4.

The baby Rabbits sing:

O little town of Bethlehem,
how still we see thee lie!
Above thy deep and dreamless
*   sleep*
the silent stars go by:
Yet in thy dark streets shineth
the everlasting Light;
The hopes and fears of all
*   the years*
are met in thee tonight.

(Philip Brooks 1835-93)

But where could they stay? The inn was full.

'Try round the back,' said the innkeeper, 'where the animals sleep.'

And there, in the stable, Jesus was born. Mary wrapped her tiny baby in swaddling clothes and laid Him in a manger.

Luke 2:5-6.

Let's sing:

Away in a manger, no crib for a bed,
The little Lord Jesus laid down His sweet head.
The stars in the bright sky looked down where He lay,
The little Lord Jesus asleep on the hay.

(Anonymous)

Just think:

Swaddling clothes are strips of cloth. Some people believe that only royal babies were wrapped in swaddling clothes.

Out in the fields around Bethlehem, shepherds were keeping watch over their sheep.

Suddenly, a bright light shone all around them and an angel appeared.

'Don't be frightened,' said the angel, (for the shepherds were terrified) 'I want to tell you some wonderful news! Your Savior—the Lord Jesus was born today in Bethlehem. And to prove it, you will find the baby wrapped in swaddling clothes and lying in a manger!'

Then a great army of angels appeared, singing praises to God.

Luke 2:8-14.

The animals are singing again:

While shepherds watched their flocks by night,
All seated on the ground,
The angel of the Lord came down,
And glory shone around.

(Nahum Tate 1652-1715)

Let's see…
A manger is a feeding trough for animals—it must have made a snug little cradle for Jesus to sleep in.

The shepherds left their sheep and
hurried off to Bethlehem. And there
they found the little Lord Jesus, just as the
angel had said.

The shepherds told Mary and Joseph about
the angels and what they had said, and Mary
remembered all these things and stored them up
in her heart. Luke 2:15-20.

Let's see…
Do you think Mary would have kept a diary?

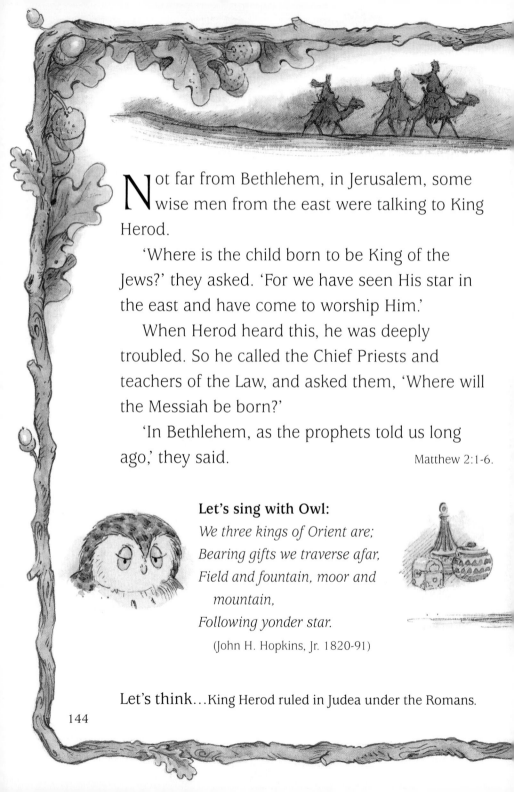

Not far from Bethlehem, in Jerusalem, some wise men from the east were talking to King Herod.

'Where is the child born to be King of the Jews?' they asked. 'For we have seen His star in the east and have come to worship Him.'

When Herod heard this, he was deeply troubled. So he called the Chief Priests and teachers of the Law, and asked them, 'Where will the Messiah be born?'

'In Bethlehem, as the prophets told us long ago,' they said.

Matthew 2:1-6.

Let's sing with Owl:

We three kings of Orient are;
Bearing gifts we traverse afar,
Field and fountain, moor and
mountain,
Following yonder star.

(John H. Hopkins, Jr. 1820-91)

Let's think…King Herod ruled in Judea under the Romans.

'When you have found the child,' Herod told the wise men, 'let me know where He is, so that I, too, may worship Him.'

As the wise men left Herod's palace, something wonderful happened. The star they had seen in the east suddenly appeared before them! And it went on ahead of them and led them to baby Jesus!

After the wise men had worshiped Jesus and given Him gifts of gold, frankincense and myrrh, they returned to their own country by another route, as they had been warned in a dream not to return to Herod.

Matthew 2:7-12.

Let's think…

Gold for a King. Frankincense for a Priest. Myrrh for a Savior.

When Herod realized he had been tricked, he was furious and gave orders to his soldiers to kill all the baby boys in Bethlehem.

But an angel had warned Joseph in a dream,

'Quick, get up!' he said. 'Take baby Jesus and His mother and escape to Egypt! For Herod is out to kill the child!'

Joseph got up right away and left that very night with Mary and baby Jesus and escaped to Egypt, where they stayed until Herod died.

Matthew 2:13-18.

Let's think…
Herod was probably frightened that one day Jesus would be King and take over his throne.

After Herod's death, the angel spoke
to Joseph again,

'Take the child and His mother, and
go back to the land of Israel. For those who
tried to kill the child are dead!'

So Joseph took his little family back home to
Nazareth, and Jesus became known as a 'Nazarene.'"

When Owl had finished reading, the baby rabbits
were tucked up in their little beds. Later that night,
when everyone was asleep, Owl helped Badger with
his deliveries. He flew on ahead, holding a lamp,
while Badger, dressed in his Santa Claus outfit,

popped a present in the stockings of all their little
friends in Oaktree Wood. Matthew 2:19-23.

Jesus of Nazareth

"**M**edicine time!" said Owl, as he popped a spoonful of nettle juice into Mole's hot little mouth. Poor Mole was not feeling very well. He had a chill and had not left his bed for a week.

"Ugh!" said Mole. "It tastes awful!"

"Well, it wouldn't be medicine if it tasted nice, now would it?" said Owl.

"Never mind," laughed Squirrel, "I've nearly got your dinner ready, that'll take the taste away!"

Squirrel and Owl had been coming in every day to look after Mole, and Mouse had not left his side.

Just then, Badger arrived with a bunch of bluebells, which he had gathered from his garden in Oaktree Wood. He had to duck down as he came through the door because Mole's house was too small for him to stand up in.

"Poor old Moley," he said, as he sat down in a chair beside the bed.

"Shall I read you a story to help cheer you up?"

"Oh, yes please, Badger," said Mole. "Can we have the one about Jesus making people better?"

"Our story begins," said Badger, "when Jesus was twelve years old.

'Where is He?' cried Mary. 'I can't find Him anywhere!' Mary and Joseph were frantic. They were on their way home from Jerusalem where they had been celebrating the Passover Festival. Lots of their friends and relations were traveling with them and they thought that Jesus was among them.

'No one has seen Him all day!' said Joseph. 'We'll just have to go back to Jerusalem and search for Him there!'

Three days later, Mary and Joseph found Jesus in the temple, sitting with the teachers.

He was listening to them and asking questions. And the teachers were asking Him questions, too.

Say a prayer with Mole:
Lord, thank you for families,
For loved ones who care,
For kindness and warmth
That families share.

Let's think…
It is about 65 miles from Nazareth to Jerusalem.

They were astonished at His answers
and His understanding.

'Jesus!' cried Mary. 'We've been worried sick!
What on earth are you doing here? Why didn't
you come home with us?'

'Why were you worried?' asked Jesus. 'You must
have guessed that I'd be here—in my Father's house!'

Luke 2:41-52.

Say a prayer with Mouse:
Help me to learn my lessons,
*   Lord,*
As Jesus used to do,
For He listened to His teachers
And His parents, too.

Let's think…
Who was Jesus' Father?

151

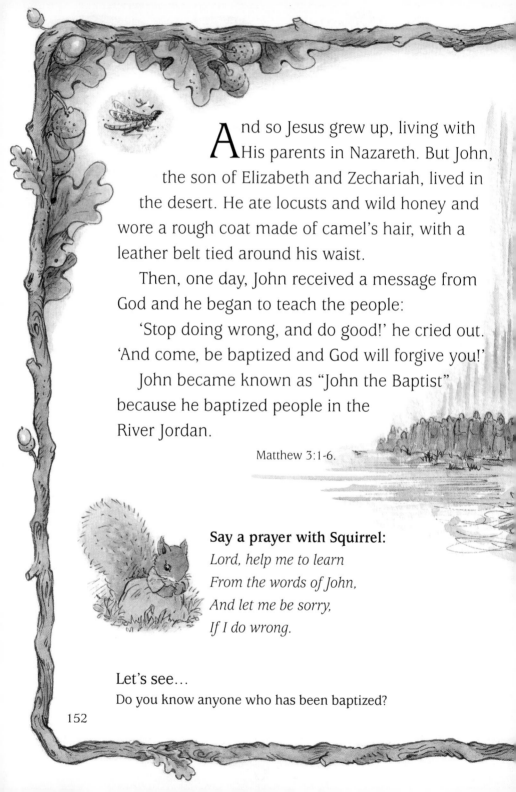

And so Jesus grew up, living with His parents in Nazareth. But John, the son of Elizabeth and Zechariah, lived in the desert. He ate locusts and wild honey and wore a rough coat made of camel's hair, with a leather belt tied around his waist.

Then, one day, John received a message from God and he began to teach the people:

'Stop doing wrong, and do good!' he cried out. 'And come, be baptized and God will forgive you!'

John became known as "John the Baptist" because he baptized people in the River Jordan.

Matthew 3:1-6.

Say a prayer with Squirrel:
Lord, help me to learn
From the words of John,
And let me be sorry,
If I do wrong.

Let's see…
Do you know anyone who has been baptized?

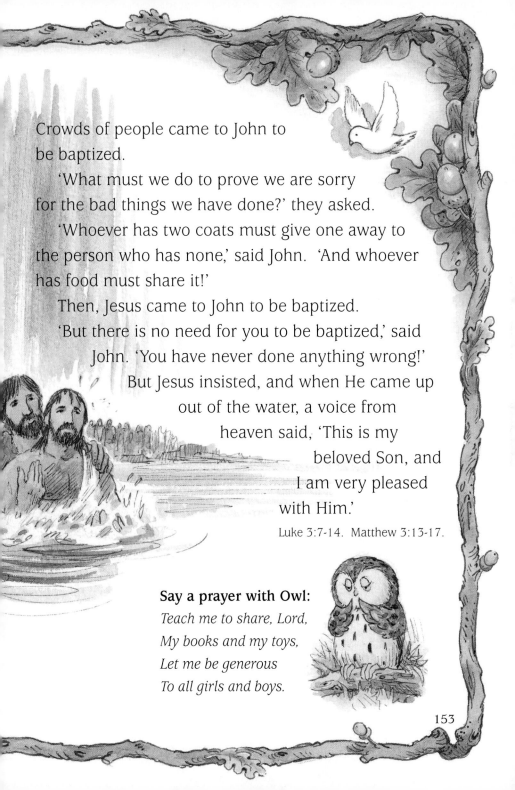

Crowds of people came to John to
be baptized.

'What must we do to prove we are sorry
for the bad things we have done?' they asked.

'Whoever has two coats must give one away to
the person who has none,' said John. 'And whoever
has food must share it!'

Then, Jesus came to John to be baptized.

'But there is no need for you to be baptized,' said
John. 'You have never done anything wrong!'

But Jesus insisted, and when He came up
out of the water, a voice from
heaven said, 'This is my
beloved Son, and
I am very pleased
with Him.'

Luke 3:7-14. Matthew 3:13-17.

Say a prayer with Owl:
Teach me to share, Lord,
My books and my toys,
Let me be generous
To all girls and boys.

Then Jesus went out into the desert and did not eat for forty days. When He was feeling very hungry, the Devil came to Him and said,

'If you are God's Son, make these stones turn into bread!'

'No!' said Jesus. 'Man can't live on bread alone. He must live as God tells him.'

Satan the Devil tried hard to make Jesus do wrong, but in the end, Jesus told him, 'Get lost, Satan!' and the Devil had to go. Then angels from heaven came and helped Him.

Matthew 4:1-11.

Badger says:
*Say 'No!' when others
want you to do something
wrong.*

Let's see…
Other names for the Devil: the enemy; the father of lies;
the evil one; the prince of demons; the great dragon;
the old serpent.

Then Jesus went back to the town
of Capernaum, to a house on the shores
of Lake Galilee. As He walked along the
beach, He saw two fishermen with a net,
catching fish. They were brothers, called Peter and
Andrew.

'Come with me!' Jesus called to them, 'and I will
teach you how to catch men!'

Immediately, Peter and Andrew left their nets and
followed Jesus.

Further along the beach, Jesus saw two more
fishermen, named James and John. They were in their
boat with their father, Zebedee. Jesus called to them, and
at once they left their boat and their father and followed
Jesus. In all Jesus called twelve men to be His disciples.

Matthew 4:12-21. 10:2-4.

Let's see…
The disciples were like students. Jesus taught them for three years—the
length of time that students today attend college or university.

155

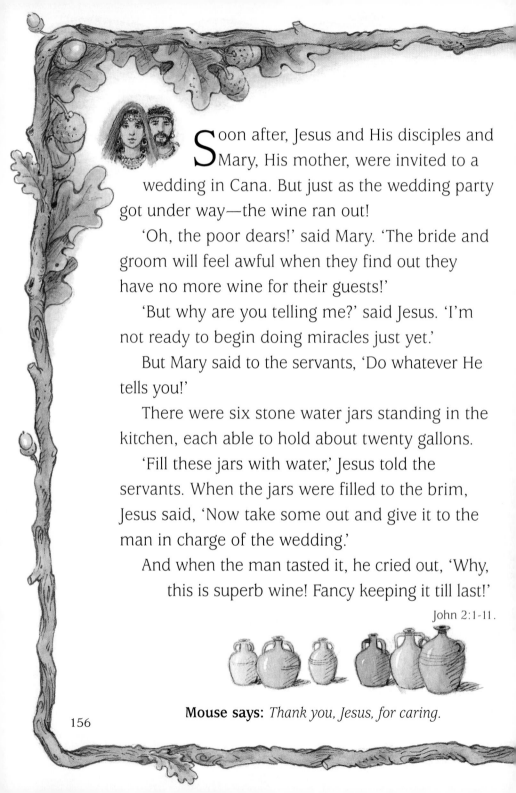

Soon after, Jesus and His disciples and Mary, His mother, were invited to a wedding in Cana. But just as the wedding party got under way—the wine ran out!

'Oh, the poor dears!' said Mary. 'The bride and groom will feel awful when they find out they have no more wine for their guests!'

'But why are you telling me?' said Jesus. 'I'm not ready to begin doing miracles just yet.'

But Mary said to the servants, 'Do whatever He tells you!'

There were six stone water jars standing in the kitchen, each able to hold about twenty gallons.

'Fill these jars with water,' Jesus told the servants. When the jars were filled to the brim, Jesus said, 'Now take some out and give it to the man in charge of the wedding.'

And when the man tasted it, he cried out, 'Why, this is superb wine! Fancy keeping it till last!'

John 2:1-11.

Mouse says: *Thank you, Jesus, for caring.*

Jesus went all over Galilee teaching
the people, 'Love God, and love your
neighbor. And believe in me, and you shall
have eternal life!'

Crowds followed Jesus wherever He went. One day
He climbed a hill and sat down. Everyone gathered
round to hear Him teach.

'Happy are those who know they need God. For they
shall be in my Kingdom,' He said.

'Happy are those who don't think about themselves
and are humble like little children, they
shall be given the earth as their own
possession.'

Matthew 4:23-25. 5:1-11.

Mole says:

Lord, help me to learn
What you expect of me,
For I want to live
For eternity!

Let's see…
These teachings are called, 'The Sermon on the Mount'. We can read
about them in Matthew 5-7.

'Don't get angry,' said Jesus.
'You must love your enemies and pray for those who are unkind to you, then you will become the children of God.

For why should God reward you if you only love those who love you? Even wicked people do that!

Try to be perfect, as your Father in heaven is perfect.

Matthew 5:21-22, 43-48.

Owl says:
It's a tall order!
But with God all things
are possible!

When you pray,' said Jesus, 'go into
your room and pray to your Father in
secret. And your Father, who sees what is
done in secret, will reward you openly.

This is how you should pray:
Our Father in heaven,
Hallowed be your name,
Your Kingdom come,
Your will be done
On earth as it is in heaven.
Give us each day our daily bread.
Forgive us our sins
As we forgive those who sin against us.
And lead us not into temptation
But deliver us from evil.
For yours is the Kingdom, the power
and the glory
For ever and ever. Amen.'

Matthew 6:5-14.

'Don't worry about what you will eat or drink,' said Jesus, 'or how you will clothe yourselves. Look at the birds—they do not sow seeds or gather a harvest—yet your Father takes care of them all. And you are worth far more than birds!

Don't look at other people and criticize them. Then God will not criticize you! For God will dish out the same rules to you as you dish out to others.

Matthew 6:24-34. 7:1-2.

Badger says:

If you're tough on others—God will be tough on you. But if you're kind, patient and understanding to others, then God will be kind, patient and understanding to you.

Your Father in heaven longs to give you every good thing. So ask Him for what you need and He will give it you. Search and you will find what you are looking for.

Your fathers know how to give good things to you. So, just think how much more your heavenly Father knows how to give good things to you when you ask Him!'

Matthew 7:7-12.

Owl says:
Do not be afraid, little children,
For it gives your Father great pleasure
To give you the Kingdom.

Luke 12:32.

Let's think…
Jesus said: Do for others what you want them to do for you. (Matthew 7:12)

When Jesus came down from the hill, He went to Peter's house.

But Peter's mother-in-law was ill. She was lying in bed with a high fever.

Jesus touched her hand and right away the fever left her. She felt so well, she got up out of bed and began to get dinner for Jesus and His disciples.

Then, that evening, all who were sick flocked to Peter's house, and Jesus healed every one of them.

Matthew 8:14-17.

Say a prayer with Mole:
Thank you, Great One,
For your dear love,
For your healing power
That comes from above.

Let's think…After Jesus had used His power in healing people, He would go away to a place on His own to pray. (Luke 5:15-16.)

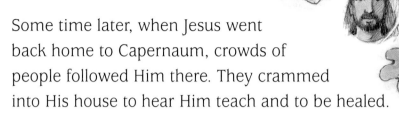

Some time later, when Jesus went
back home to Capernaum, crowds of
people followed Him there. They crammed
into His house to hear Him teach and to be healed.

As He was teaching, four men arrived carrying a
paralyzed man on a stretcher. They wanted Jesus to
heal him, but because of the crowd they could not even
get in the door! So they made a hole in the roof, right
above the place where Jesus was teaching! Carefully,
they lowered the man down. When Jesus saw their
faith, He said to the man,

'Get up! Pick up your bed and walk!'

Then, to the astonishment of all in the house, the
paralyzed man got up, took up his bed and went home.

Mark 2:1-12.

Let's think…

If the four men in the story had not been so determined, their friend
might not have been healed.

'Let's go across to the other side of Lake Galilee,' said Jesus to His disciples. So they climbed into a boat and as they were sailing, Jesus fell asleep. Suddenly, a strong wind got up and the boat began to fill with water! They were in danger of sinking!

'Jesus, wake up!' cried the disciples. 'We're all going to drown!'

'Why are you so frightened?' said Jesus. And He got up and ordered the wind and the sea to be still. And the wind and the sea obeyed Him, and there was a great calm.

The disciples were amazed."

Mark 4:35-41.

Mole says:
When troubles come upon me,
I know the Lord is near,
For He longs to help me
And take away my fear.

Let's think…
About Jesus' awesome power!

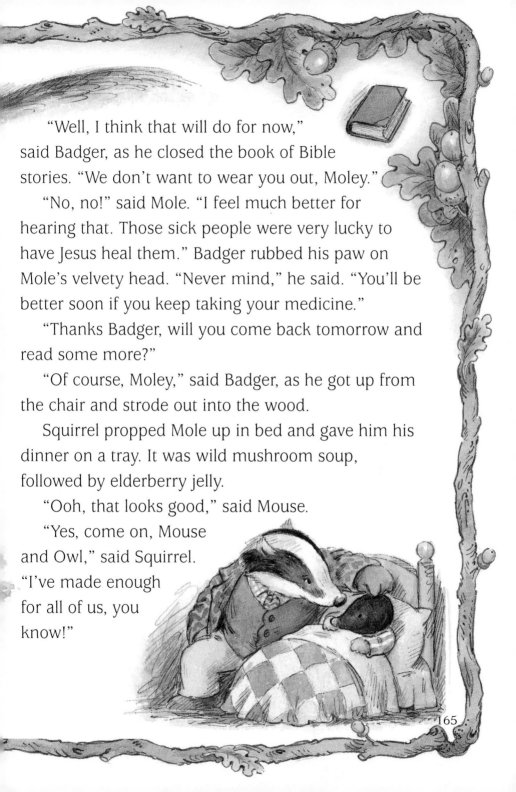

"Well, I think that will do for now," said Badger, as he closed the book of Bible stories. "We don't want to wear you out, Moley."

"No, no!" said Mole. "I feel much better for hearing that. Those sick people were very lucky to have Jesus heal them." Badger rubbed his paw on Mole's velvety head. "Never mind," he said. "You'll be better soon if you keep taking your medicine."

"Thanks Badger, will you come back tomorrow and read some more?"

"Of course, Moley," said Badger, as he got up from the chair and strode out into the wood.

Squirrel propped Mole up in bed and gave him his dinner on a tray. It was wild mushroom soup, followed by elderberry jelly.

"Ooh, that looks good," said Mouse.

"Yes, come on, Mouse and Owl," said Squirrel. "I've made enough for all of us, you know!"

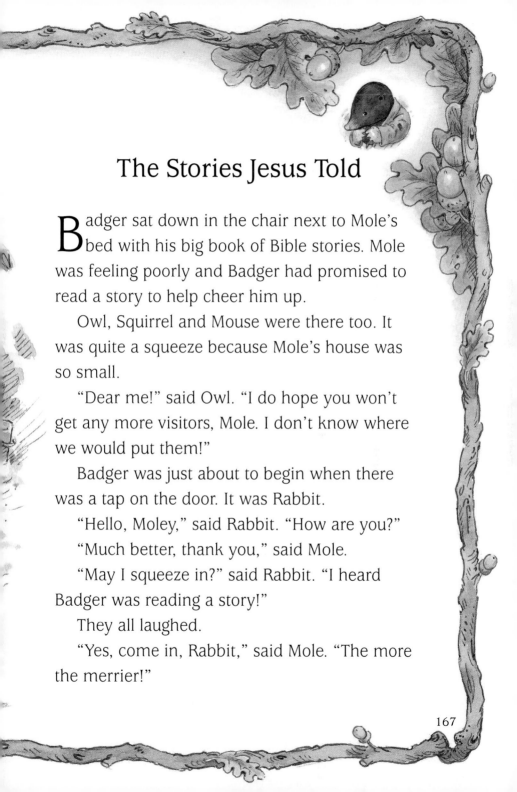

The Stories Jesus Told

Badger sat down in the chair next to Mole's bed with his big book of Bible stories. Mole was feeling poorly and Badger had promised to read a story to help cheer him up.

Owl, Squirrel and Mouse were there too. It was quite a squeeze because Mole's house was so small.

"Dear me!" said Owl. "I do hope you won't get any more visitors, Mole. I don't know where we would put them!"

Badger was just about to begin when there was a tap on the door. It was Rabbit.

"Hello, Moley," said Rabbit. "How are you?"

"Much better, thank you," said Mole.

"May I squeeze in?" said Rabbit. "I heard Badger was reading a story!"

They all laughed.

"Yes, come in, Rabbit," said Mole. "The more the merrier!"

"One day, as Jesus was walking along the sea shore," read Badger, "crowds of people came out of the towns and began to follow Him. So Jesus sat down on the sand to teach them. But the crowd grew so big, not everybody could see or hear Him. So He got into a boat on the water and taught the people from there, while they stood on the sea shore to listen.

Matthew 13:1-3.

Badger says:

Jesus often told stories to the people. These stories are called 'parables'.

Let's see…

A parable helps us to understand some of the lessons that Jesus wants us to learn.

The Story of the Sower

'A farmer went out to sow corn,' said Jesus. 'But not all the seed fell in the field. Some fell on the path where it was trod on, and the birds ate it up.

Some fell on hard, rocky ground and when the seeds sprouted, they quickly dried up and died because they had no moisture.

Matthew 13:3-6.

Sing with Squirrel:

We plough the fields, and scatter
The good seed on the land,
But it is fed and watered
By God's almighty hand.

(M. Claudius 1740-1815)

Let's think…

There were no tractors in those days, so the farmer walked through his fields carrying a bag of seed on his shoulder. And as he walked, he scattered the seed by hand over the fields.

Some of the seed fell in the hedges around the fields,' said Jesus. 'And when the plants grew up, the thorns and bushes choked them. But some of the seed fell in the good soil, where the plants grew up big and strong.'

'Tell us what the Parable of the Sower means,' said the disciples.

'All right,' said Jesus. 'I am the farmer and the seed is the word of God. The seed that fell on the path stand for those who hear my message but do not understand it. Then what they have learnt is soon forgotten.

Matthew 13:7-9, 18-19.

Say a prayer with Rabbit:
Lord, help me not to forget your words.

Let's think…
Jesus said that if we ask Him for understanding, then He will give it us.

The seed that fell on rocky ground stand for those who are happy about the message when they hear it, but they don't take it seriously, so they soon give up when things get difficult.

The seed that fell among the thorns are the people who hear the message, but they let other things in their life crowd it out.

And the seed sown in the good soil in the field are those who hear the message and understand it, and they live good lives and help others to understand it too.'

Matthew 13:20-23.

Say a prayer with Mouse:
Let me not crowd out, Lord,
The Good News that you bring,
For loving you and others
Is the most important thing.

Let's think…
It's all right to live a full life, as long as we put God's way first.

Hidden Treasure

Jesus said, 'The Kingdom of Heaven is like treasure, which a man found hidden in a field. The man was so excited, he sold everything he owned to raise enough money to get the field—and the treasure too!'

Matthew 13:44.

Badger says:
There is a box of treasure,
Hidden just for you,
It doesn't cost a penny
But its price is all of you.

Let's think…
Have you found the treasure?

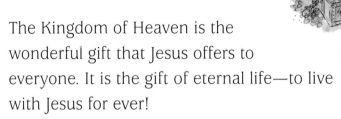

The Kingdom of Heaven is the wonderful gift that Jesus offers to everyone. It is the gift of eternal life—to live with Jesus for ever!

Those who believe that Jesus can give us this gift are like the man who finds the treasure. But to receive the gift we must love God and love others. That means we have to stop being unkind and doing bad things, which is like the man in the story who had to sell everything he owned to get the treasure. For God's treasure is so wonderful it is worth giving up everything to receive it.

Matthew 13:44-46. John 3:16. Luke 10:25-28.

Owl says:
I am making a list of
things to give up.
Can you help me finish it?
Short temper
Impatience
Telling fibs
Not keeping my word
Hooting too loudly
(or shouting at others)

173

'Who will be the greatest in the Kingdom of Heaven?' the disciples asked.

So to answer them, Jesus called a little child and stood him in front of them.

'Unless you change yourselves and become humble and trusting like this child, you will never enter the Kingdom of Heaven.'

Matthew 18:1-5.

Mole says:
Lord, help me to always love you, then I will always trust you.

Let's see...
Most little children take it for granted that their parents will feed, clothe and look after them. That's how God wants us to be with Him.

174

Then some of the people brought their children to Jesus so that He could pray for them.

But the disciples tried to shoo them away.

When Jesus saw it, He said, 'Let the children come to me!

Do not stop them, because the Kingdom of Heaven belongs to those people who have hearts as trusting as these little children.

Remember, whoever does not have their kind of faith, will never enter my Kingdom.'

Luke 18:15-17.

Squirrel says:
Faith is believing God, even though it cannot yet be seen what He promises!

Let's think…
Jesus loves little children.

175

The Lost Sheep

Jesus told this story because he overheard a finely dressed Pharisee complain:

'Look at Jesus! He talks to all the down-and-outs and those who don't keep our religious rules! He even eats with them!'

'A man had a hundred sheep,' said Jesus. 'But one of them got lost. So the man left the ninety-nine sheep in the field and went searching for the lost sheep until he found it.

Then he put it on his shoulders and carried it back home. He was so happy, he called in his friends and neighbors to celebrate.

Luke 15:1-6.

Let's see…
The Pharisees were a group of people who lived by a set of rules and regulations. They thought it was more important to keep these rules than to lend a helping hand to those in need.

176

In the same way,' said Jesus. 'There will be more happiness in heaven when one lost person—one of these down-and-outs—returns to God, than over ninety-nine other good people who do not need to repent.'

Also Jesus told the Pharisee the story of the Lost Son (or Prodigal Son). The father in the story is like our Father in heaven. He longs to help every one of us and will not turn anyone away, no matter what he or she has done.

Luke 15:7.

Owl says:
The Lord loves us, and everyone,
No matter what we've said or done.

Let's think…
Every single person is precious to God.

The Prodigal Son

'There was once a man who had two sons,' said Jesus. 'One day the sons would inherit all that their father owned. But the younger son could not wait.

"Father, let me have my share of the money now!" he said. So the father divided his property between his two sons.

Then the younger son went off and wasted all his money. He became so poor he had nowhere to live and nothing to eat. The only job he could find was feeding the pigs. He was so hungry, he nearly ate the pigs' food!

Luke 15:11-16.

Rabbit says:

Sometimes, dear Lord, we're foolish,
We do such silly things,
We forget the pain and hardship—
The tears that badness brings.

At last he came to his senses. "What am I doing here?" he said. "I will go back home and tell my father I'm sorry. Perhaps he will let me be one of his workers, for they all have plenty to eat!" So he set off for home, and while he was still a long way off, his father ran out to meet him.

"Dad, I've been so stupid!" he said. "I don't deserve to be called your son. Please, let me be your servant!"

But the father would not hear of it. He dressed the boy in new clothes, put shoes on his feet and a ring on his finger. Then he called everyone in to celebrate. For he said, "This my son was lost but now he is found!"'

Luke 15:17-24.

Squirrel says:
*If everything goes wrong,
And you don't know what to do,
There's one who longs to help—
He's waiting there for you.*

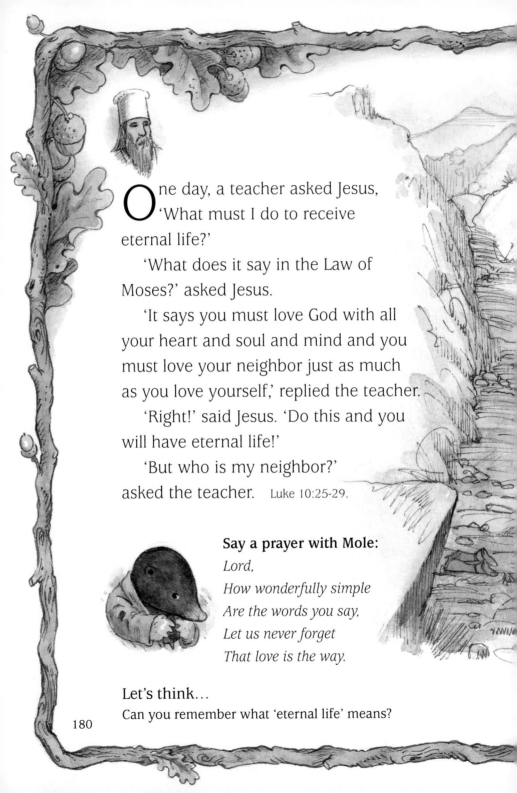

One day, a teacher asked Jesus, 'What must I do to receive eternal life?'

'What does it say in the Law of Moses?' asked Jesus.

'It says you must love God with all your heart and soul and mind and you must love your neighbor just as much as you love yourself,' replied the teacher.

'Right!' said Jesus. 'Do this and you will have eternal life!'

'But who is my neighbor?' asked the teacher.   Luke 10:25-29.

Say a prayer with Mole:
Lord,
How wonderfully simple
Are the words you say,
Let us never forget
That love is the way.

Let's think…
Can you remember what 'eternal life' means?

The Good Samaritan

To help the teacher to understand, Jesus told him this story.

'A man was walking from one town to the next, when bandits attacked him. They stripped him of his clothes and money, beat him up and left him half dead by the roadside.

By chance, a priest came along and saw him. But he crossed over to the other side and did nothing to help.

Then another religious person came along and he too walked on by.

Luke 10:30-32.

Say a prayer with Rabbit:

When others are in trouble,
And I hear their urgent cry,
Even if I'm busy, Lord,
I will not walk on by.

Let's think…

The priest and religious person may have thought that it was more important to get to church on time than to help the injured man.

181

At last, a Samaritan—a foreigner—saw him and was filled with pity. He cleaned and bandaged his wounds. Then he put the man on his own donkey and took him to an inn, where he looked after him.

The next day he gave some money to the innkeeper.

"Take care of him," he said. "And if you spend any more on him, I will pay you when I return."'

Luke 10:33-35.

Say a prayer with Mouse:
Lord,
Thank you for those who
give
Kindness and love,
Their goodness and
patience
Come from above.

Let's think…

This part of the story must have been difficult for the Pharisee, because the Pharisees in Jesus' time hated the Samaritans.

Then Jesus said to the teacher,
'Now which of these three would you say acted like a neighbor to the injured man?'
'The one who was kind to him,' said the teacher.
'Yes!' said Jesus. 'Now go and do the same!'"

"They were great stories," said Mole. "Thank you, Badger, for reading them. Now I think I can understand the type of person God wants us to be!"

"Yes," smiled Badger, as he tucked Mole up in his little bed. "Just like you, Moley!"

Luke 10:36-37.

Jesus and His Friends

Mole, who had been feeling poorly lately, was better at last. He was so happy to be out and about again, he decided to invite all his friends to a barbecue beneath the trees in Oaktree Wood.

Badger was busy stoking the fire with his stick, and Squirrel was making sure that the chestnuts

did not burn. Mouse was munching on roasted hazelnuts and Rabbit was helping himself to a large lettuce salad.

"I just want to thank you all for looking after me during my illness," said Mole. "I don't know what I would have done without you. You are the best friends anyone could ever wish for!"

"Ah, that reminds me," said Badger. "The story for today is called 'Jesus and His Friends.' Would you like to read it, Owl? I want to make sure the barbecue doesn't go out!"

"I should be delighted," said Owl.

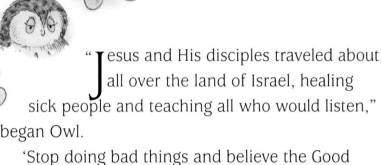

"Jesus and His disciples traveled about all over the land of Israel, healing sick people and teaching all who would listen," began Owl.

'Stop doing bad things and believe the Good News!' said Jesus. The Good News is that God has made a way for us to be forgiven for the bad things we do. So all we have to do is ask God to forgive us—and He will! But that is not all! There is even more Good News! God has been busy preparing something wonderful for all of us—a place in His Kingdom!

Matthew 11:4-5.

Say a prayer with Squirrel:

Lord, you love me dearly,
That is plain to see,
For in your heavenly Kingdom,
You've made a place for me!

Let's think…
Has anyone ever forgiven you for something you did wrong?
It's good to be forgiven.

'There are many rooms in my Father's house,' said Jesus. 'And I am going to prepare a place for you. I wouldn't tell you this if it wasn't true. And after I've prepared a place for you, I will come back and welcome you into my home, so that where I am, you may be also.'

John 14:2-3.

Mole says:
*I'm going to live with Jesus
One happy, happy day.
I'm going to live with Jesus,
He's said that I can stay.*

Let's see…
Don't you think that this is the best news ever?

Jesus and His disciples sometimes went to the capital city, Jerusalem, where Jesus would teach the people in the Temple.

But one day, He found that traders had filled the Temple Courts. Also moneychangers (who were not very honest) were sitting at tables changing people's money into the coins for the Temple tax.

John 2:13-14.

Say a prayer with Mouse:
Lord Jesus we thank you,
That your house is where,
Your people can gather
For praise and for prayer.

Let's think…
Around the Temple buildings in Jerusalem, were courtyards where people could gather for prayer and teaching.

Jesus knew that the traders should not have been there. The Temple Courts were meant to be quiet places where strangers and people from different lands could go and pray. He was so upset, He sat down and made a simple whip. Then He got up and drove out the animals. He overturned the tables of the moneychangers and the stools of those who sold doves.

'Take them out of here!' He cried. 'Stop making my Father's house a market place! It is written in the Scriptures that God said, "My Temple will be called a house of prayer for the people of all nations." But you have made it into a den of thieves!'

John 2:15-17. Isaiah 56:7.

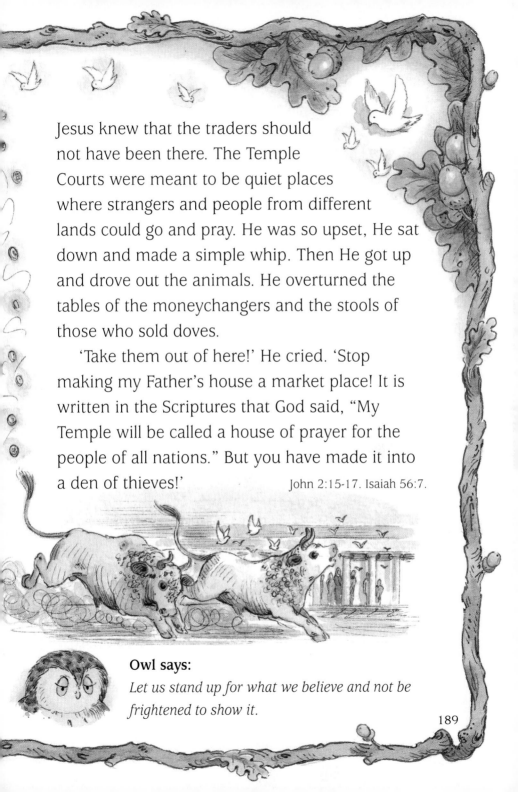

Owl says:

Let us stand up for what we believe and not be frightened to show it.

'I am the Light of the World!' said Jesus. 'Whoever follows me will never walk in the dark but will live his life in the light.'

John 8:12.

Badger says:

*If you find it hard
To believe that God is there,
Ask the Lord to show Himself.
He wants to hear your prayer.*

Let's see...

All who follow Jesus will have a purpose to their lives. They will understand why we are here and what life is about. Many people don't understand this, because thy refuse to believe in God and the words of Jesus. Jesus said that living your life like this is like trying to find your way in the dark.

'I am the Good Shepherd,' said Jesus. 'I will always look after the sheep. I know my sheep and my sheep know me. My sheep listen to my voice. I know them and they follow me. I give them eternal life and they shall never die. No one can take them away from me.'

John 10:11,14,15,27,28.

Mouse says:

I am Jesus' little lamb,
And He loves me so,
He leads me and I follow,
Wherever He may go.

Let's think…

In the time of Jesus, the fields were not fenced, so the sheep needed a shepherd to keep them from straying and to keep them safe from thieves and wolves.

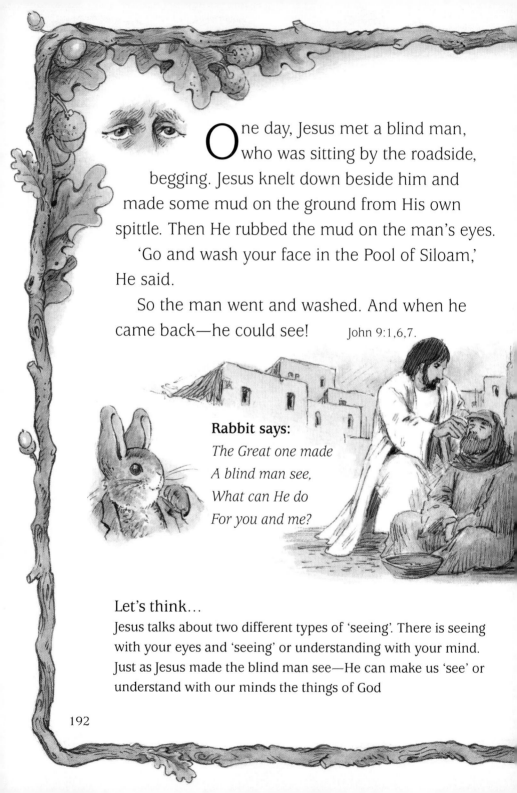

One day, Jesus met a blind man, who was sitting by the roadside, begging. Jesus knelt down beside him and made some mud on the ground from His own spittle. Then He rubbed the mud on the man's eyes.

'Go and wash your face in the Pool of Siloam,' He said.

So the man went and washed. And when he came back—he could see!   John 9:1,6,7.

Rabbit says:
*The Great one made
A blind man see,
What can He do
For you and me?*

Let's think…
Jesus talks about two different types of 'seeing'. There is seeing with your eyes and 'seeing' or understanding with your mind. Just as Jesus made the blind man see—He can make us 'see' or understand with our minds the things of God

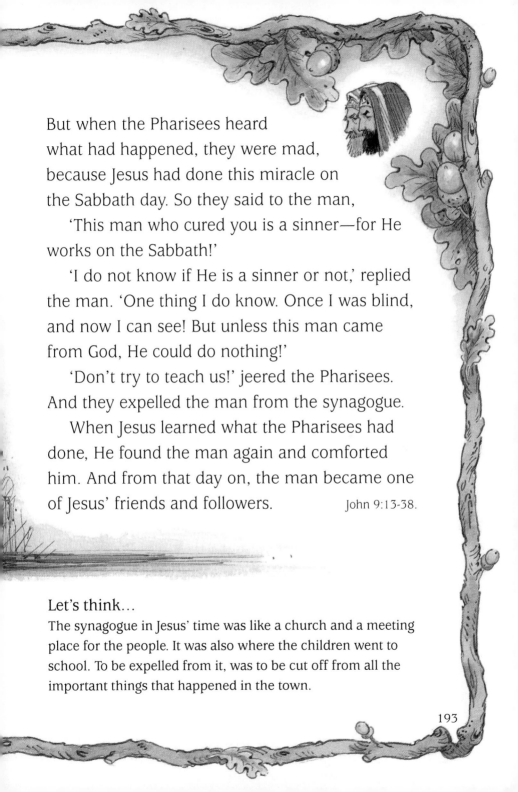

But when the Pharisees heard
what had happened, they were mad,
because Jesus had done this miracle on
the Sabbath day. So they said to the man,

'This man who cured you is a sinner—for He
works on the Sabbath!'

'I do not know if He is a sinner or not,' replied
the man. 'One thing I do know. Once I was blind,
and now I can see! But unless this man came
from God, He could do nothing!'

'Don't try to teach us!' jeered the Pharisees.
And they expelled the man from the synagogue.

When Jesus learned what the Pharisees had
done, He found the man again and comforted
him. And from that day on, the man became one
of Jesus' friends and followers.   John 9:13-38.

Let's think...

The synagogue in Jesus' time was like a church and a meeting
place for the people. It was also where the children went to
school. To be expelled from it, was to be cut off from all the
important things that happened in the town.

Jesus often went to stay with his friends, Mary, Martha and Lazarus, who lived in Bethany, a village near Jerusalem. 'Lovely to see you again, Jesus,' said Martha. 'Do come in, and all your disciples too. Sit down and rest while Mary and I get you something to eat.'

Luke 10:38.

Owl says:

It's good to often visit
The friends you love the best,
Where you can sit in comfort
To talk and to rest.

Mole says:

Thank you, Lord, for my friends.

But oh, dear, Mary would not help Martha to get the dinner ready! For Jesus had begun to teach His disciples, and Mary found it so interesting, she just had to sit down and listen. Poor Martha was upset. She had so much to do and there were so many people to cook for, and only her to do it! At last she went to Jesus.

'Lord, my sister has left me to do all this work by myself!' she complained. 'Tell her to come and help me!'

Luke 10:39-40.

Say a prayer with Squirrel:
Lord, help me to sit and listen,
As Mary used to do,
To hear the old, old story,
That is forever new.

Let's see…
Do you think it was unkind of Mary not to help her sister?

'Martha! Dear Martha!' said Jesus. 'You are worried and bothered about doing so many things. But only one thing is really needed. And Mary has chosen that one thing and it must not be taken away from her!'

Luke 10:41-42.

Say a prayer with Mouse:

Lord, help me to know what is really important.

Let's see…Do you think that Martha left the cooking and sat down next to Mary to listen to Jesus?

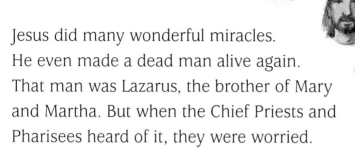

Jesus did many wonderful miracles.
He even made a dead man alive again.
That man was Lazarus, the brother of Mary
and Martha. But when the Chief Priests and
Pharisees heard of it, they were worried.

'What shall we do?' they cried. 'Look at all the
miracles this man is performing! If we let Him go on
like this, everyone will believe in Him. Then we shall
have the Romans on us and that will be the end of
our Temple and our nation!'

And so, from that day on, the authorities
planned to kill Jesus. But Jesus kept out of their way.

'If anyone knows where Jesus is,' ordered the
Chief Priests, 'it must be reported, so we can arrest
Him!'   John 11:45-48,53,54,57.

Say a prayer with Mole:
*Lord, help all grown-up people who find
it hard to put their trust in you.*

Let's see…
Do you think the Pharisees were right to be worried?

Soon after, Jesus went to dinner again with Mary, Martha and Lazarus, where He knew He would be safe. While they were eating, Mary poured a pound jar of very expensive perfume on Jesus' feet! Then she wiped His feet with her hair. The whole house was filled with the sweet smell of the perfume. John 12:1-3.

Say a prayer with Badger:

Lord, let me not forget,
That the little things I do,
Mean an awful lot,
To others and to you.

Let's think…

Jesus said that all over the world, wherever the Gospel is preached, what Mary has done will be told in memory of her. (Matthew 26:13)

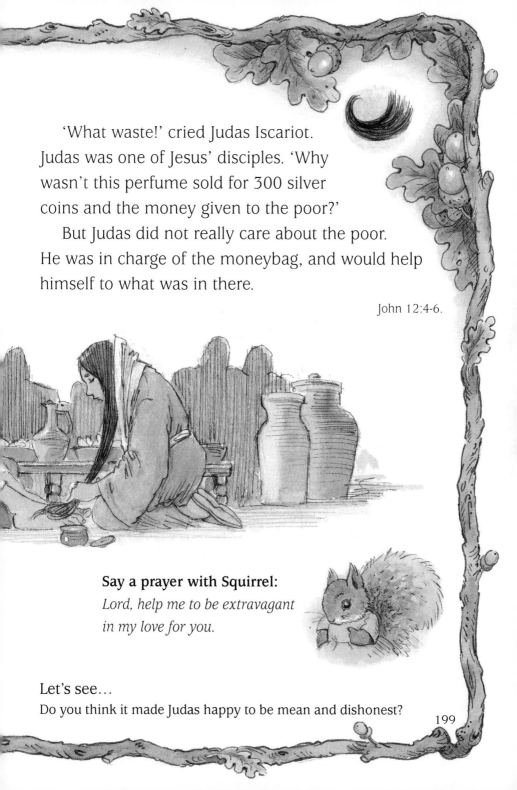

'What waste!' cried Judas Iscariot.
Judas was one of Jesus' disciples. 'Why
wasn't this perfume sold for 300 silver
coins and the money given to the poor?'

But Judas did not really care about the poor.
He was in charge of the moneybag, and would help
himself to what was in there.

John 12:4-6.

Say a prayer with Squirrel:
*Lord, help me to be extravagant
in my love for you.*

Let's see…
Do you think it made Judas happy to be mean and dishonest?

'Leave her alone!' said Jesus. 'She has saved this perfume for the day of my burial. You will always have the poor with you, but you will not always have me!' "

John 12:7-8.

Say a prayer with Badger:
Lord Jesus, you are precious,
More than words can say,
I want to give you honor
Each and every day.

Let's think…
What Mary did is remembered more than any words she said.

"It's a great barbecue, Moley," said Mouse, as Owl came to the end of the story. "I shall always remember it!"

"And I will always remember the way you all helped me when I was ill," said Mole.

"Yes, it's good to remember," said Owl.

"And it's good to have friends, too!" said Mole, as he topped up everyone's cup with elderberry tea.

Jesus says Goodbye

Squirrel had just finished packing away her winter stores. She had collected so many acorns that fall that she didn't know what to do with them all. So she decided to invite all her friends in Oaktree Wood to a Harvest Party.

Owl was the first to arrive. Badger was next.

"Ho! Ho!" he laughed, as he helped Mouse, Mole and Rabbit climb up to the top of the Great Oak Tree where Squirrel lived. "Squirrel's house is so high, it's like climbing up to heaven!"

"Do you remember that story about Jesus— when He went up to heaven?" said Mouse, after they had admired Squirrel's store cupboards.

"Yes, but I'd like to hear that one again," said Rabbit.

"Will you read it to us, Badger?" asked Squirrel, as she cut them all a large slice of acorn cake.

"Of course," said Badger. "But it is a very sad story, so you must promise me that you'll remember there is a happy ending!"

"We promise," said everyone.

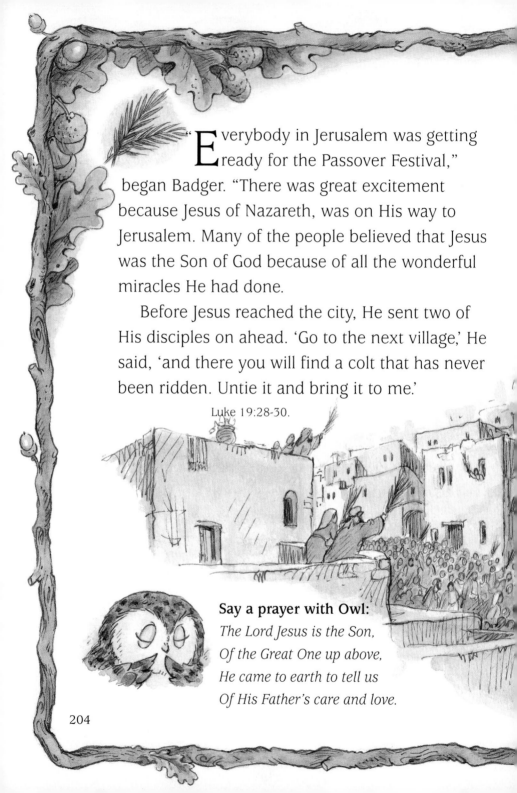

"Everybody in Jerusalem was getting ready for the Passover Festival," began Badger. "There was great excitement because Jesus of Nazareth, was on His way to Jerusalem. Many of the people believed that Jesus was the Son of God because of all the wonderful miracles He had done.

Before Jesus reached the city, He sent two of His disciples on ahead. 'Go to the next village,' He said, 'and there you will find a colt that has never been ridden. Untie it and bring it to me.'

Luke 19:28-30.

Say a prayer with Owl:
The Lord Jesus is the Son,
Of the Great One up above,
He came to earth to tell us
Of His Father's care and love.

The disciples brought the colt to Jesus then threw their coats over it. Jesus got on, and rode into Jerusalem. Many people spread their coats on the road ahead of Him and others cut down palm branches and spread them on the road. When Jesus came into Jerusalem, the whole city exploded with excitement.

'Hooray for Jesus!' shouted the crowds. 'God bless the Son of the Great One!'

But the Pharisees said, 'Look! The whole world is following Him! We must stop Him!'

Matthew 21:1-11.

Let's see…

What do you think usually happens when someone gets on a young male horse that has never been ridden before?

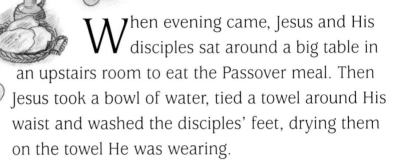

When evening came, Jesus and His disciples sat around a big table in an upstairs room to eat the Passover meal. Then Jesus took a bowl of water, tied a towel around His waist and washed the disciples' feet, drying them on the towel He was wearing.

'The leader among you must be like a servant,' said Jesus.

'I am your leader, but I have washed your feet. So you should wash one another's feet.'

John 13:4-17.

Say a prayer with Mole:
Help me, Lord, to serve others.

Let's think...
When people came into a house in Jesus' time, it was the job of the lowliest servant to wash their dusty feet.

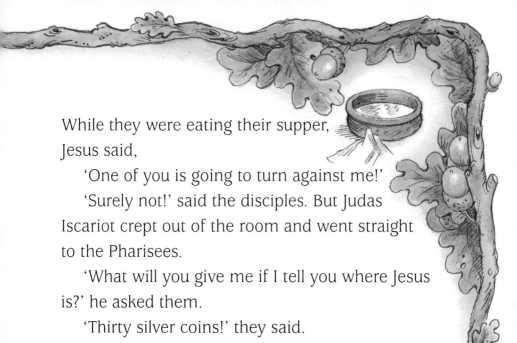

While they were eating their supper,
Jesus said,

'One of you is going to turn against me!'

'Surely not!' said the disciples. But Judas
Iscariot crept out of the room and went straight
to the Pharisees.

'What will you give me if I tell you where Jesus
is?' he asked them.

'Thirty silver coins!' they said.

After Judas had left, Jesus took some bread and
wine and gave them to the disciples.

'Every time you eat this bread and drink this
wine,' He said, 'You must remember the New
Agreement I am going to make for you.'

John 13:21-30. Matthew 26:14-16,26-30.

Let's think…

The New Agreement is between God and every man and
women, girl and boy: God will agree to forgive the wrong things
we do, and give us eternal life, if we agree to follow Jesus.

'Listen!' said Jesus. 'Here is a new commandment for you! Love one another! As I have loved you, so you must love one another. If you have love for one another, then everyone will know that you are my followers. If you love me, you will keep my commandments. My Father in heaven will love whoever loves me and I too will love him.'

John 13:34-35. 14:15,21.

Sing with Squirrel:

Jesus loves me! This I know,
For the Bible tells me so;
Little ones to Him belong;
They are weak, but He is strong.

'When I am taken away from you,' said Jesus, 'I will ask the Father to send you a special helper, called the Holy Spirit.'

'Lord, I would rather die than let anyone take you away from us!' said Peter.

'I tell you, Peter,' said Jesus. 'Before the rooster crows this morning, you will say three times that you do not know me!'

John 14:16-17,26. 13:37-38.

Let's think…

The Holy Spirit is a special gift given to the followers of Jesus. It's like having a secret friend who helps, guides and comforts us all through our lives.

Jesus loves me! He will stay
Close beside me all the way;
Then His little child He'll take
Up to heaven, for His dear sake.

(Anna Warner 1827-1915)

Then Jesus went out into the dark night with His disciples to a quiet garden to pray.

Soon after, Judas arrived with a gang of armed soldiers and guards, carrying torches and lanterns. The Chief Priests and Pharisees had sent them. (Judas had given them a signal: the one I kiss is the man you want!) Immediately, Judas went up to Jesus and kissed Him.

Then the Roman soldiers arrested Jesus, tied Him up, and took Him away to the High Priest's house.

Matthew 26:47-49,57.

Mouse says:
Lord, I'm awful sorry this happened to you.

Let's think...
When someone betrays a person today, we sometimes say, he gave him 'The Kiss of Judas.'

Peter followed on behind and went into the garden of the High Priest's house.

'This man was with Jesus!' said one of the servant girls, when she saw Peter.

'But I don't even know Him!' said Peter.

'You are one of His followers!' a man said.

'I am not!' said Peter.

'But you're from Galilee!' said another man. 'You must have been with Jesus!'

'I don't know what you're talking about!' said Peter.

Suddenly, a rooster crowed. Then Peter remembered what the Lord had said, and he went outside and cried his heart out.

Luke 22:54-62.

Let's see…Why do you think Peter cried?

211

The Chief Priests tried to find someone to say something bad about Jesus, but nobody could find any wrong in Him. Jesus was questioned all night, but He would not make any reply.

At last, the High Priest said, 'Tell us, are you the Son of God?'

'Yes, I am!' said Jesus.

At this, the High Priest tore his clothes in fury.

'Wicked lies!' he cried. 'You deserve to die!'

Then early in the morning, they put Jesus in chains and led Him to Pilate, the Roman governor.

Matthew 26:57,63-66. 27:1-2.

Badger says:
Our Lord, like a lamb,
Was quiet and meek,
He kept silent
And would not speak.

Pilate knew that the Chief Priests
had handed Jesus over to him
because they were jealous, so he tried
hard to set Jesus free. But the Chief Priests
and elders were determined to have Jesus put
to death, and they got the people to cry out:
'Crucify Him! Crucify Him!'

Then Pilate was frightened there would be a riot,
so he took a bowl of water and washed his hands
in front of the crowd.

'I want nothing to do with the death of this just
man,' he said. 'This is your doing!'

Matthew 27:11-12,18,22-25. John 19:12.

He was mocked and jeered
All night long,
Yet He did not cry out,
Nor do any wrong.

Let's think…
Pilate knew it was wrong to put Jesus to death, so he "washed
his hands" of the whole business.

213

Then they led Jesus away and crucified Him. 'Father, forgive them,' prayed Jesus. 'For they don't know what they are doing!'

Standing by the cross were Mary, Jesus' mother, and John, the disciple. When Jesus saw them, He said, 'Mother, this is your son.' Then He said to John, 'Look! This is your mother!' And from then on, John took Mary into his own home and looked after her.

Luke 23:34. John 19:25-27.

Owl says:
*Even when the Lord
Suffered upon the cross,
He still could think of others
And of their pain and loss.*

From twelve noon to three in the afternoon, it was dark over all the land. Then Jesus called out in a loud voice, 'It is finished!' And He bowed His head and died.

Suddenly, the earth shook. Rocks split open. And the huge curtain in the Temple was torn in two from top to bottom.

When the soldiers saw and heard what had happened, they were terrified, and said, 'This man really was the Son of God!'

Matthew 27:46.

Let's think…

Sin, or the bad things we do, separates us from God. But now, because Jesus died, our sins can be forgiven, so we can be close to God.

Rabbit says:

Hooray!
Now we can all be at one,
With each other, with God,
And with His Son!

A rich man named Joseph, who was a secret follower of Jesus, asked Pilate if he could take Jesus' body away. Another man, called Nicodemus, helped him. The two men wrapped Jesus' body in linen cloths then placed it in Joseph's own tomb. Before they left, they rolled a great stone across the entrance.

Some of the women from Galilee sat outside the tomb, watching.

John 19:38-42.

Rabbit says:

Lord, let me not be frightened,
Or fear what some may say,
Because I follow Jesus,
And want to live His way.

Let's see…

Both Joseph and Nicodemus had been too frightened of the Chief Priests and Pharisees to follow Jesus openly. Do you think they were still frightened?

The Pharisees sealed the tomb and put a guard outside, in case the disciples should steal Jesus' body away and say He had risen from the dead.

Then early on Sunday morning, Mary Magdalene and another woman went to the tomb.

Suddenly, there was a great earthquake. And an angel came down from heaven and rolled the stone away. His face shone as bright as lightning.

'Don't be frightened,' he said to the women. 'I know you are looking for Jesus. But He is not here. He has come back to life again!'

The guards were petrified and could not move for fear.
Matthew 27:62-66. 28:1-8.

Let's think…
One day there will be no more death, or sadness, or crying.
(Revelation 21:4)

217

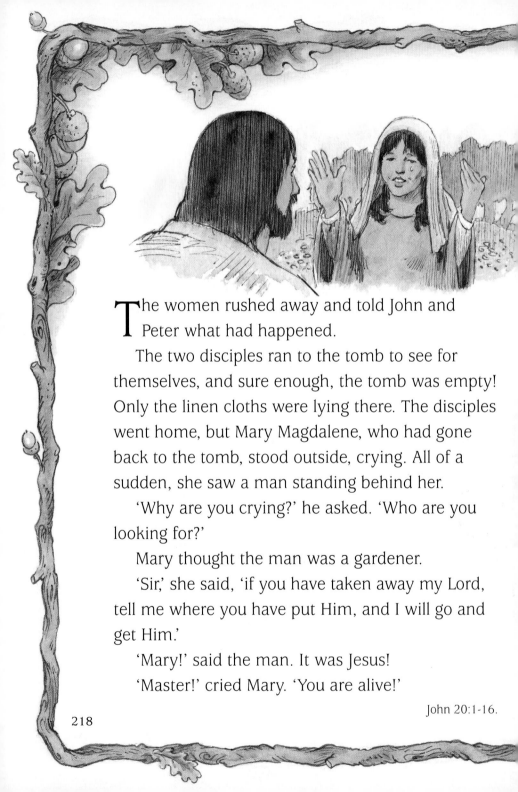

The women rushed away and told John and Peter what had happened.

The two disciples ran to the tomb to see for themselves, and sure enough, the tomb was empty! Only the linen cloths were lying there. The disciples went home, but Mary Magdalene, who had gone back to the tomb, stood outside, crying. All of a sudden, she saw a man standing behind her.

'Why are you crying?' he asked. 'Who are you looking for?'

Mary thought the man was a gardener.

'Sir,' she said, 'if you have taken away my Lord, tell me where you have put Him, and I will go and get Him.'

'Mary!' said the man. It was Jesus!

'Master!' cried Mary. 'You are alive!'

John 20:1-16.

218

After that, Jesus met and spoke
with His disciples many times.

Then at last the time came for Him
go to His Father. The disciples stood
watching. Then suddenly, two men appeared,
dressed in white.

'Why are you looking up at the sky?' they asked.
'For Jesus, who has been taken up from you into
heaven, will one day come back in just the same
way as you have seen Him go!' "   Acts 1:9-11.

"Were the two men, angels?" asked Mouse.

"Yes, I think so," said Badger, when he had
finished reading.

"Sometimes, angels help people," said Mole.

"Well, I think an angel must have helped me this
fall," laughed Squirrel. "That's why I found so many
acorns!"

Good News

"Bother this weather!" said Rabbit! "I hate it when it rains! It's so boring—you can't do anything!"

"We could go and visit Badger," said Squirrel. "Maybe he will read us a story!"

Rabbit and Squirrel had planned to go blackberrying. But it was too wet for that.

"If it doesn't stop soon, all the blackberries will spoil!" said Rabbit, as they made their way to Badger's house.

"Ho, ho!" said Badger, when he saw the wet pair. "Come in and get yourselves dry. You're just in time, for Mouse, Mole and Owl are already here and I'm about ready to begin reading them a story. It's a very exciting one, so it will help to cheer you all up!"

"The story begins soon after Jesus was taken up to heaven," said Badger.

" 'Listen!' cried Mary. 'What's that noise?'

'I—I don't know!' replied John. 'It sounds like a great, rushing wind!'

Suddenly, one of the women screamed. And the strange, mighty wind filled the whole room where the disciples and the followers of Jesus were meeting for prayer.

Then, all of a sudden, there appeared flames, like tongues! And before anyone could do anything, the tongues of fire spread out and touched each person in the room!

Acts 2:1-3.

Say a prayer with Mole:
Let your Holy Spirit
Touch me, Lord, I pray,
Fill me with your love,
Every single day.

Then something amazing happened.
Each person began to speak in a foreign
language! They were all filled with the Holy
Spirit!

Lots of people from foreign lands were staying
in Jerusalem at that time, and when they heard
the great commotion that the followers of Jesus
were making, they rushed over to see what was
happening.

Acts 2:4-6.

Let's think…

Before Jesus went back to heaven, He promised His followers
that He would send them the gift of the Holy Spirit (a kind of
invisible friend) who would help them to live the way that
Jesus had taught them.

223

'What's going on?' cried an Egyptian man. 'I come from Egypt, yet I can hear one of these men from Galilee talking about Jesus in my own language!'

'And I can hear one of them speaking about Jesus in Greek!' said a woman from Greece.

All the foreign people living in Jerusalem could hear the Good News in their own language! They were all astonished.

'What on earth does this mean?' they cried.

Acts 2:7-12

Let's think...
The Lord wants everyone, no matter who they are or where they come from, to understand the Good News. Today, the Bible is printed in many different languages.

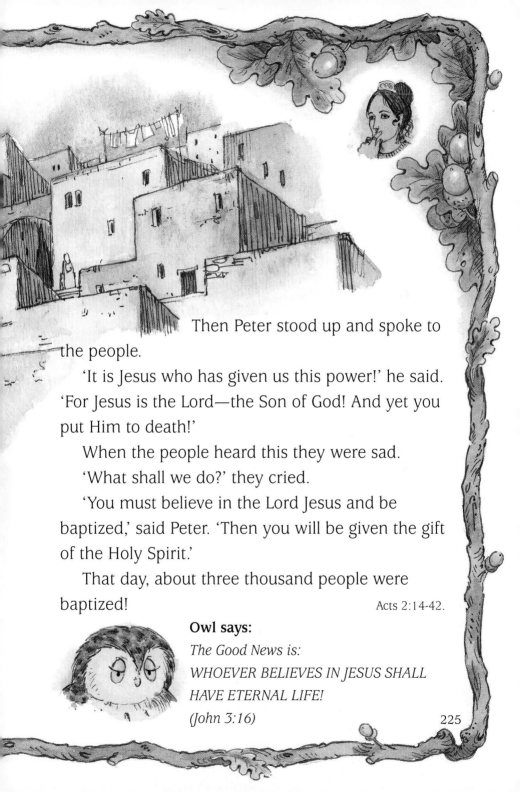

Then Peter stood up and spoke to the people.

'It is Jesus who has given us this power!' he said. 'For Jesus is the Lord—the Son of God! And yet you put Him to death!'

When the people heard this they were sad.

'What shall we do?' they cried.

'You must believe in the Lord Jesus and be baptized,' said Peter. 'Then you will be given the gift of the Holy Spirit.'

That day, about three thousand people were baptized!

Acts 2:14-42.

Owl says:

The Good News is:
WHOEVER BELIEVES IN JESUS SHALL
HAVE ETERNAL LIFE!
(John 3:16)

The disciples did many wonderful miracles, and the people loved them.

Every day new believers were baptized. They all wanted to learn about Jesus, so they met with the disciples each day in the Temple Courts. They shared their meals together and were very happy. They even sold their houses and the things they owned and divided the money out between them. Nobody was in need.

Acts 2:43-47.

Say a prayer with Rabbit:
Lord, help me to learn
To share and to give,
To those in need
Wherever they live.

Let's think…
We all need to learn as much as we can about Jesus.

One day, when Peter and John went to the Temple, they saw a man who could not walk. He was begging for money.

'Please, can you spare a few coins?' the beggar asked them.

'I have no money,' Peter said. 'But what I have, I will give you. In the name of Jesus of Nazareth, I order you to get up and walk!'

At once, the man's legs and feet became strong. He jumped up and walked into the Temple, giving thanks to God.

Acts 3:1-10.

Squirrel says:
Remember! Remember!
Now you have been told,
The words of Jesus
Are better than gold!

Crowds of people from the city and from outside Jerusalem brought their sick to the disciples, and every one was healed.

This made the High Priest and elders very jealous, so they had the disciples arrested and put in jail.

'You are not to teach about Jesus!' they said.

But in the middle of the night, an angel of the Lord opened the prison gates and led the disciples out.

'Go to the Temple and tell everyone about this new life!' he said.

Acts 5:16-20.

Mouse says:
If you love God, then you will love others,
For they are your sisters and brothers.

Let's think…
Let us be happy when others do well.

The next morning, the High Priest arrived at the Temple and called together all the elders. Then he sent soldiers to the jail to fetch the disciples for questioning. But when the soldiers got there, the prison was empty! So they went back to the High Priest.

'When we got to the jail, it was locked up all right,' they said. 'The guards were on duty outside. But when we opened the gates, there was nobody inside!'

Acts 5:21-23.

Badger says:
No matter how bad things are,
The Lord can make them better.

'The men you put in prison are teaching in the Temple Courts!' a man told the elders.

'Go and fetch them!' ordered the High Priest.

So the soldiers brought the disciples back and made them stand before the court of elders.

'We gave you strict orders not to teach the people about Jesus!' they said. 'But you have spread your message all over Jerusalem!'

Acts 5:25-28.

Owl says:
*Lord, when we believe
That your way is true,
We want to tell others
What you can do.*

'We must obey God rather than men!' said Peter. 'That is why we tell people about Jesus. For Jesus is our Savior. He loves and cares about us and wants us to live with Him forever!'

This made the members of the court so furious they had the disciples whipped.

'You are not to speak in the name of Jesus again!' they ordered. But every day the disciples went to the Temple Courts and to the believers' homes to tell them the Good News about Jesus.

Acts 5:29-42.

Let's see…
If you learn some good news, what is the first thing you want to do? Share it!

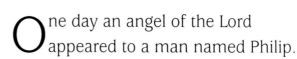

One day an angel of the Lord appeared to a man named Philip.

'Go to the desert road—the one that runs south from Jerusalem,' said the angel.

So Philip went, and on his way he met an Ethiopian, who was an important official of Queen Candace of Ethiopia. The man was sitting in his chariot, reading from the book of Isaiah in the Bible:

> *He was led away like a lamb,*
> *But He did not open His mouth,*
> *And His life was taken away from the earth.*

Acts 8:26-33.

Let's think...

Isaiah wrote this more than seven hundred years before the birth of Jesus!

'Who is this person that Isaiah is talking about?' asked the Ethiopian.

'He is talking about Jesus!' said Philip.

Then the Ethiopian asked Philip to come up and sit with him in his chariot. And as they went along, Philip told him the Good News about Jesus. Soon, they came to some water.

'Look!' said the Ethiopian. 'Here is some water. Can I be baptized?'

So Philip baptized him, and as they came up out of the water, the Spirit took Philip away to another place. The Ethiopian never saw him again, but he went on his way, full of happiness.

Acts 8:34-40.

Let's think…

I wonder how many people learnt about Jesus in Ethiopia, after that!

233

Later, King Herod began to trouble some of the people who belonged to the church. He arrested Peter and put him in jail. Sentries stood on guard at the prison gate, and sixteen soldiers guarded him! At night he slept between two guards and was tied up in chains. But the people of the church were praying hard for Peter.

Acts 12:1-5

Say a prayer with Badger:
*Thank you, Lord, for those
Who care enough to pray,
For those who are in trouble,
Or upset in any way.*

Suddenly, as Peter lay sleeping,
an angel appeared in the prison cell
and filled it with light. He shook Peter's
shoulder.

'Quick!' he said. 'Get up!' At once, the chains
fell off Peter's hands.

'Put on your cloak and sandals,' said the angel.
'And follow me!' Peter thought he must be
dreaming, as he and the angel left the prison cell
and passed by the guards who were on duty.

'This can't be true,' he said to himself, when the
iron gate that led into the city, strangely opened
for them by itself! Acts 12:6-10.

Squirrel says:

Ask and it shall be given to you,
Seek, and you will find,
Knock and it shall be opened up
*   for you,*
For your heavenly Father is so kind.
(Luke 11:9-10)

As Peter and the angel walked down the street, suddenly the angel disappeared.

'Wow!' said Peter. 'I'm not dreaming! The Lord sent His angel to rescue me—and I'm free!'

Quickly, Peter made his way to a friend's house, where many believers had gathered to pray for him. He knocked at the door, and a servant girl named Rhoda came to answer it.

'Hey, let me in!' called Peter.

Acts 12:10-13.

Mouse says:
Don't be surprised,
When God answers prayer,
For He longs to help
Those in His care.

When Rhoda heard Peter's voice, she was so excited she ran back in without opening the door.

'Peter's at the door!' she cried out.

'Don't be mad!' they said. 'How can he be?'

'But he is, I heard him!' she cried.

'He can't be! He's in jail!' they said. 'It must be his angel!' But Peter kept knocking at the door. And at last they opened it. And there he was! They could hardly believe their eyes!"

Acts 12:14-16.

"Look!" cried Rabbit, when Badger had finished reading. "It's stopped raining!"

"Then let's go blackberrying!" said Squirrel.

"Hey—can me and Moley come too?" asked Mouse.

" 'course you can," said Rabbit.

And that night, before she went to bed, Squirrel made a large blackberry pie especially for Badger, to thank him for reading them the Good News story.

Paul's Adventures

Mouse and Mole and their friends were sailing their toy boat on the pond in Oaktree Wood. Suddenly, a gust of wind blew it against a big rock and it capsized.

"Oh, dear!" cried Mole.

"Shipwreck!" shouted Mouse.

"Ho! Ho!" laughed Badger, as he waded into the water to rescue the boat for his little friends. "I know a good story about a shipwreck. When you've finished playing I'll read it to you!"

"Oh, read it now, please Badger," cried Mouse and Mole together.

"The story begins," said Badger, "when the disciples were hard at work in Jerusalem, teaching everyone about Jesus.

'Believe in the Lord Jesus, and follow Him and you shall be given the gift of eternal life,' they cried.

Many of the people believed, and there were now lots of Christians living in Jerusalem. But there was one man they all feared. His name was Paul. Paul hated Christians. He went from house to house dragging out the believers, and throwing them into jail.

Acts 8:1-3.

Say a prayer with Mole:
Lord, those who love you
Can rightly claim,
They share with you
Your own dear name.

Let's think…
A Christian is someone who follows Jesus Christ.

All the believers, except the disciples, were so frightened of Paul, they packed up their bags and left Jerusalem. Many of them went north to a city called Damascus.

But Paul went after them. He had permission from the High Priest to arrest all the men and women in Damascus who believed in Jesus, and bring them back in chains to Jerusalem.

Acts 9:1-2.

Badger says:

Those who choose to do what's wrong,
Are cut off from God's love,
They cannot know the kindly Friend
Who watches from above.

Let's think…

Paul was an important Pharisee and very well educated.

But something very strange happened to Paul when he was on the road to Damascus. As he came near to the city, suddenly a dazzling light from heaven shone down on him. He fell to the ground, blinded. Then he heard a voice.

'Paul, Paul, why are you persecuting me?' it said.

'Who—who are you?' cried Paul.

'I am Jesus, the one you are persecuting!' said the voice.

Paul was so frightened, he began to tremble all over.

'What do you want me to do, Lord?' he asked.

Acts 9:3-6.

Owl says:

Watch out! Things will change when the Lord takes a hand in your life.

242

'Go into the city,' said Jesus. 'And you will be told what to do!'

The people traveling with Paul led him into Damascus. He was blind for three days. Then God spoke to a man named Ananias in a dream.

'Go to Paul and heal him, for he is blind,' He said.

'But Lord,' said Ananias, 'Paul is a terrible person. He is persecuting the Christians and throwing them all into jail!'

'Go,' said the Lord. 'For I have chosen Paul to be my special servant.'

So Ananias went to Paul and said, 'Brother Paul, see again!'

Acts 9:6-18.

Let's think...

Can you guess the first thing Paul did when he could see again? Yes, he was baptized!

243

Immediately, Paul began to teach that Jesus is the Son of God. The people in Damascus were amazed.

'Isn't this the man who was arresting all the Christians?' they asked. 'What's happened to him?'

But the priests and elders said, 'We'll have to get rid of Paul. He's too clever!' So they kept watch, day and night, at the city gates, hoping to capture him.

Acts 9:20-23.

Let's think…
Cities in those days were surrounded by big, strong walls, so it would be easy to spot anyone going in or out of the gates.

'You must get out of Damascus!' the Christians told Paul. 'Some of the priests and elders are after you!'

'I'll go to Jerusalem,' said Paul, 'and join the disciples!'

That night, the Christians helped Paul to escape. They lowered him down in a basket over the city wall. And so Paul was able to leave the city in safety. When he arrived in Jerusalem, the disciples were afraid of him.

'Paul will put us all in jail,' they said. But when they saw what a change had come over him, and that he now believed in the Lord Jesus, everyone was happy, and the church had peace at last.

Acts 9:24-25.

Mouse says:
Love changes everything.

Paul, and another believer, named Silas, went to many different countries, teaching people everywhere about Jesus, and setting up churches. Then one day, while they were in Greece, some men got mad at Paul and Silas and had them arrested. The magistrate ordered them to be beaten and then thrown into jail.

'Guard them with your life!' he told the jailer. So the jailer locked them up in a cell deep inside the prison. He put chains on their hands and clamped their feet in the stocks.

Acts 16:22-24.

Let's see…
Stocks are specially shaped wooden blocks of wood. They were used to clamp the feet of prisoners, to stop them from escaping.

That night, Paul and Silas prayed
from their prison cell and sang hymns
to the Lord. All the other prisoners were
listening.

Then all of a sudden, a great earthquake shook
the whole building. The doors of the cells flew
open and the chains that were holding the
prisoners, fell off.

Acts 16:25-26.

Rabbit says:
Whenever I'm in trouble,
Upset or feeling blue,
I will sing my favorite hymns,
Out loud, dear Lord, to you.

Suddenly, the jailer woke up and saw all the prison doors wide open.

'Oh, dear!' he cried. 'The prisoners have escaped! What shall I do? The magistrate will kill me for this!'

'It's all right,' called Paul. 'We are all here!'

The jailer could not believe it. He grabbed a light and rushed to the cell. Trembling with fear, he fell down before Paul and Silas.

Acts 16:27-29.

Squirrel says:
The Great One is a God of miracles and wonders!

The jailer led the two men out of prison.

'Sirs,' he said. 'What must I do to be saved?'

'Believe on the Lord Jesus,' they said, 'and you will be saved. You and all your family!'

Then Paul and Silas told the jailer and those who were in his house, all about Jesus. The jailer was overjoyed.

'I am so sorry you were beaten,' he cried, as he washed their wounds. 'Please forgive us!'

'The Lord Jesus forgives all who are sorry for the wrong things they do,' said Paul. Then the jailer and all his family were baptized.

Acts 16:30-34.

Let's see...
What do you think 'being saved' means?

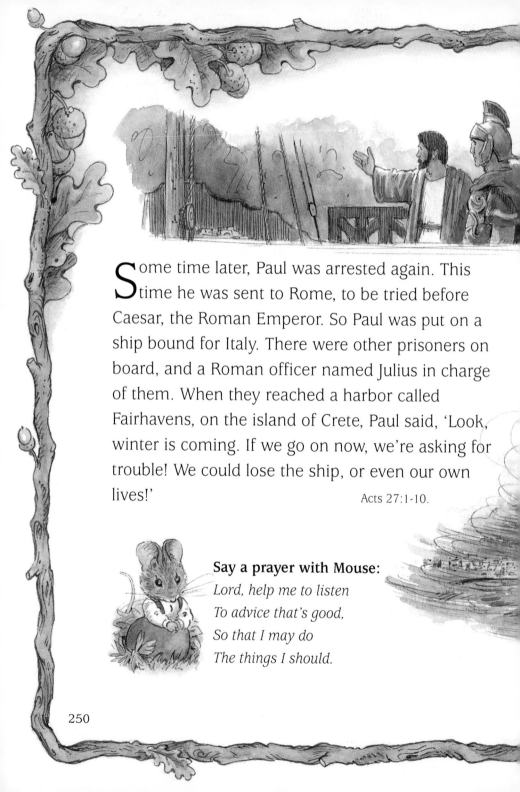

Some time later, Paul was arrested again. This time he was sent to Rome, to be tried before Caesar, the Roman Emperor. So Paul was put on a ship bound for Italy. There were other prisoners on board, and a Roman officer named Julius in charge of them. When they reached a harbor called Fairhavens, on the island of Crete, Paul said, 'Look, winter is coming. If we go on now, we're asking for trouble! We could lose the ship, or even our own lives!'

Acts 27:1-10.

Say a prayer with Mouse:

Lord, help me to listen
To advice that's good,
So that I may do
The things I should.

Julius and the captain of the ship
paid no attention to Paul.

'I don't want to spend the winter in
this harbor,' said the captain. So they went
on. But soon after they set sail, a strong wind
got up and blew the ship off course—out to the
open sea.

The sailors tried hard to head back for shore,
but it was impossible.

'Help! We're going to capsize!' they cried. So
they threw the cargo overboard, to help lighten
the ship. Next day they threw out the tackle and
anything else they could find.

Acts 27:11-19.

Let's see…
What do you think Paul was doing while all this was going on?
What would *you* do?

The terrible storm raged on for days. Thick black clouds blotted out the sun and the stars. Everyone gave up hope of being saved—except Paul.

'Cheer up!' he said. 'God has promised me that nobody is going to lose his life, even though the ship will go down!'

Then, at last, they spotted land. But before they could reach it, the ship began to break apart.

'All those who can swim must jump overboard,' ordered Julius. 'Then all the rest of you must follow. Grab whatever you can find and paddle ashore the best you can!'

And so, what Paul said came true, and everyone escaped safely to shore!

Acts 27:20-44.

Say a prayer with Badger:

Lord, guard those who sail at sea,
And bring them safely home again,
Where they are glad to be.

They soon learned they were on the island of Malta.

'Brrr!' cried the shipwrecked sailors. 'We're cold!'

So the islanders built a fire on the beach to warm the cold survivors.

Publius, the Roman governor of the island, took them all back to his home. While they were there, they discovered that Publius' father was ill. So Paul prayed for him, and he was made better. Then all the other sick people on the island came to Paul, and they were all healed. The islanders were so grateful, they showered the travelers with gifts when they set sail again."

Acts 28:1-10.

Owl says:
All things turn out right in the end when we trust the Lord.

"Well, Paul got safely to Rome," said Badger, "and while he was there, he wrote lots of letters to the churches which he'd set up. Some of the letters are in our Bible. One of the most well known is found in 1 Corinthians 13, it is about love, and this is it," said Badger.

Love is patient and kind,
it is never jealous or envious,
never boastful or proud.
It is never selfish or rude.
There are three things
that are more important than
    anything else:
faith, hope and love,
and the greatest of these is
    love.

1 Cor. 13:4-5,13

254

"The last book in the Bible is called Revelation," said Badger. "It's a book about the future—what will be. Here are some of the things it says:"

… Look! Now God has made His home with mankind! He will live among them, and they shall be His people. God Himself shall be with them, and He will be their God. He will wipe away all tears from their eyes. There will be no more death, nor sorrow, nor crying. There shall be no more pain, for all those old things are past and gone. (Rev. 21:3-4)

Listen!' says Jesus. 'I am coming soon!' (Rev. 22:12)

…So be it, Come, Lord Jesus! (Rev. 22:20)

"Is that the very end of the book?" asked Mouse, when Badger had finished reading.

"Yes, it is!" said Badger. "The very end!"

"Well, it is a very happy ending," said Mole. "I like it!"